The Spice Companion

The Spice Companion

Sarina Kamini

Copyright © 2022 Sarina Kamini

All rights reserved. No part of this book may be reproduced or transmitted in any form or by any means, electronic or mechanical, including photocopying, recording, or by any information storage and retrieval system, without permission in writing from the copyright owner.

Disclaimer: All information and material in this book is for informational purposes only. If you have allergies or food intolerances to any products mentioned in this book, please do not consume. Neither the author or publisher shall be liable for any negative consequences to anyone reading or following the information in this book.

Publishing Details

SK Publishing

Publisher: SK Publishing
Website: www.sarinakamini.com

Cover Design: Melinda Childs
Interior and cover layout: Pickawoowoo Publishing Group -
www.pickawoowoo.com
Illustrations: Toshi Singh.

A catalogue record for this book is available from the National Library of Australia

ISBN 978-0-6455850-0-1 (paperback)
ISBN 978-0-6455850-5-6 (hardback)
ISBN 978-0-6455850-1-8 (ebook)

ALSO BY SARINA KAMINI
Spirits in a Spice Jar

www.sarinakamini.com

For Scott, Cailean, Ash, and Chip Dog.
The most important people in my life.
My world's magic because you're all in it.

Contents

Introduction · 1
Welcome To The Spice Companion · · · · · · · · · · · · · 3

East vs West · 9
An Inclusive Spice Framework · · · · · · · · · · · · · · · ·11

The Palate · 15
What Is The Palate ·17

Spice Categories · 23
A World Beyond Recipe · · · · · · · · · · · · · · · · · · · 25
Acidic Spice · 27
Astringent-Sulphuric Spice · · · · · · · · · · · · · · · · · 29
Bitter Spice · 30
Earth Spice ·32
Forest Floor Spice · 33
Hot Spice · 34
Structural Spice · 36
Sweet Spice ·37

Warm Spice · 39
Salt · 40

Fats · **43**
Flavour Influencers · 45
Coconut Oil · 46
Ghee · 48
Macadamia Oil · 50
Mustard Oil · 52
Olive Oil · 54
Peanut Oil · 56
Sesame Oil · 58
Yoghurt · 60

Spices · **65**
Spice Terminology · 67
Ajwain · 72
Amchur · 74
Aniseed · 76
Aniseed Powder · 78
Asafoetida · 80
Bay Leaf · 83
Indian Bay Leaf · 85
Cardamom Black · 87
Cardamom Green · 89
Cardamom Green Powder · · · · · · · · · · · · · · · 91
Cassia Bark · 94
Cassia Powder · 97

The Spice Companion

Cayenne Pepper · 100
Chilli Powder Kashmiri · · · · · · · · · · · · · · · · · · · 102
Chilli Powder Red · 105
Cinnamon Powder · 107
Cinnamon Quill · 110
Coriander Leaf · 112
Coriander Powder · 115
Clove Buds · 118
Clove Powder · 121
Cumin Powder · 123
Cumin Seed · 125
Curry Leaf · 127
Fennel Powder · 129
Fennel Seed · 132
Fenugreek Leaf (Dried) · · · · · · · · · · · · · · · · · · · 135
Fenugreek Powder · 138
Fenugreek Seed · 141
Galangal Fresh · 143
Galangal Powder · 145
Garam Masala · 147
Garlic Fresh · 150
Ginger Fresh · 152
Ginger Powder · 154
Jaggery · 156
Lemon Fresh · 159
Lime Fresh · 161
Mace Flower · 163
Mace Powder · 165

Mustard Seed Black · 168
Mustard Seed Yellow · 170
Nigella Seed · 172
Nutmeg Powder · 175
Onion Fresh · 178
Pepper Black · 181
Pepper White · 184
Pepper Szechuan · 186
Pomegranate Molasses · 188
Saffron · 190
Salt Indian Black · 192
Salt Fine Pink · 195
Salt Fine White Sea · 197
Sumac · 199
Tamarind · 201
Turmeric Fresh · 203
Turmeric Powder · 205

Acknowledgements · **209**
Author · **211**

Introduction

Welcome To The Spice Companion

I HAVE A SINGULAR MEMORY of shelling peas with my Ammie in New Delhi that I've turned over in my mind so many times I no longer know which parts are real and which are embellished.

In one version I am sitting on a cold concrete step beside her and I can smell that smell that is so peculiar to an Indian kitchen in winter: concrete, and water, and residual heat from the last meal. The sun is shooting a shaft of light to warm us. In another I think I must have imagined that step and instead we are perhaps in her small front garden, cane chairs on a square of concrete that cuts in a sharp line to fresh lawn.

But certain aspects of that memory are fixed. It was winter. I was very young. We were shelling peas. And for that moment in time I was all hers and Ammie was all mine. Ammie was my Kashmiri Pandit grandmother and it's from her lineage that my work with spice springs. Just not in the way you imagine.

Nostalgia can be a trap in food culture. I didn't get around to establishing my own Indian kitchen until my early thirties. When I did my fixation on recreation made the process far more fraught than it had to be. I wanted my dal to taste like Ammie's. My paneer to taste like Mum's. My lamb to taste like Dad's. It drove me wild that I couldn't match the memories—even with their recipes on hand.

Eventually I realised the common denominator at the heart of all my "mistakes" was the taste of me. I used salt differently to Ammie. Chilli and cinnamon powder differently to Dad. And I had a generosity of hand with fats that didn't belong to Mum. Until then I didn't understand how *sentient* an ingredient could be: how much a spice or a fat responds to the way it is handled. I realised that in the space between the flavours I remembered and the flavours I was making was a whole bunch of information that could help me understand spices better. I realised I had to get to know each aromatic, each fat, each piece of produce individually.

I did it via full immersion. I cooked every. single. day. And wrote reams on every piece of information about spice and about me that I discovered. It helped that food and its communication has always been my profession: I've spent 25 years working as a food writer, critic, and food journalist across three continents and five countries. This work cooking, deconstructing, and writing about my spices eventually formed the basis of a memoir, Spirits In a Spice Jar, that was published in 2018.

But honestly the biggest shift to understanding spice happened when I started sharing it. In 2017 in small-town Margaret River, a friend gathered a group together, put money in my bank account, and forced me to come teach. I didn't believe her when she said that what I knew about spices might be worthwhile to others. I was ridiculously nervous: how was I ever going to communicate to these people everything that I knew and loved about spice? It mattered *sooo* much to me that the information should have value. Value to my students, I mean. I already knew of its value to me. So I designed a way of speaking, and thinking about, and framing spice that gave my students contextual understanding of how I grew up with it. This was important to establish an understanding of what spice can mean traditionally. And then I broke down that context. Lightening up the Indian-ness of it. The me-ness of it. Because it turns out that the key ingredient in understanding individual spices lies not in tradition or nostalgia, but in loosening the tight frames of cultural context.

Now as a food communicator, educator, and author, I zero in on the "you-ness" of the spices that you are using. I do it by asking you to leave aside what you know, and using your sensory abilities to start a new kind of relationship to these foods: one that is broad, and that takes in spice function, aromatic categorisation, and *possibilities*.

There are so many great **what-ifs** with spices. What if... I use green cardamom pods in my tomato and white wine mussels. What if... I sprinkle chilli, fennel seed, and turmeric through my salt and pepper scrambled eggs. If I were standing beside you in the kitchen, this is the information on spice, fats, and spice usage that I would share.

I go as softly as I can—I've learned through my work teaching classes that spice can feel prohibitive. Some of the information is a little technical just because it's such a complex food. I give helpful definitions in the following pages so you might find the language that I use around spice simpler to navigate. And I've worked to provide entrance points of understanding for all people at all levels as we proceed to breakdown each spice throughout the Companion. I talk about when a spice can be tricky to get right: ajwain, for example, or even clove buds in a savoury context. Or when a known "sweet" spice might be used in a savoury context: like cinnamon powder. These comments are included so you might move a little more thoughtfully. If you're *still* nervous then to you I'd say—don't worry too much about getting things wrong. Remember it's only food. It's only a dish. Just one meal. Getting a handle on new ways to use spice requires failure in order to understand our own limits. I know that I always love when a dish works out just the way I'd hoped. Just as I understand that I always learn when it doesn't.

Spices are how my Kashmiri family loves. As a Kashmiri-Australian woman I get the benefit of straddling two worlds and that's how I've come to present spice to my students. It's given me so much joy to find a space within spices that I reside: cooking has become an act of discovery, and sharing the food that I cook a true expression of joy given to feed those that I love. It's for this reason that I hope my book becomes a stained mess of well-leafed pages on your kitchen benchtop. A reference you go back to again and again as you get drawn deeper into this fascinating aromatic world. The simplest way to a happy life is appreciation of simple pleasures. Ultimately this is part of what spice has become for me. And it's for this reason that I hope you might find as much to love in spices as I do.

East vs West

Indian Spices

+

Western cuisine

An Inclusive Spice Framework

THE KEY WORK I DO in teaching spice is breaking down the traditional framework around "Indian" aromatics and re-introducing them into modern and Western contexts. When I first started teaching spice classes in 2017 I pretty quickly realised how foreign "Indian" spice seemed to Western audiences: most of my students were intimidated by spices, the complexity around blending, and the sheer number of individual aromatics. Up until that point I didn't realise that the idea of cooking with spice could be prohibitive. For me, it had always been like coming home. And I guess I wanted to share my feeling of connection with the people cooking with me.

So the way that I've come to teach is to use my connection, to open yours. Each spice and fat catalogued in this Companion is turned like a jewel: I will show you the facet of Indian tradition, sometimes my own personal relationship to an aromatic, and then I will tilt the spice so that it can be seen through the prism of Western culinary culture.

And that's why I put quote marks around "Indian" aromatics. In fact, it goes to the heart of this explanation and of this Companion: spice isn't "Indian" any more than butter is French, or chickpeas are Lebanese. Sure, the French use butter to make a mean *beurre blanc*. And chickpeas are the pre-requisite for the hummus that presents at every Lebanese table. And certain spices are commonly layered in the Indian dishes I grew up making. But that doesn't mean you have to cook in the French style to use butter. Or that you can only use cumin in a masala.

The secret of your ability is to use spice like you. This is the only way the learning really sticks for most people. Getting to use turmeric powder in your chicken soup, or black cardamom in your béchamel, or amchur on your roast vegetables creates an intimacy over time. You begin to understand the flavours, the character, the texture, and the potential of the spices that you use. You begin to build a relationship with spice "like an Indian" but the conversation occurs in your own language. Your children / family / friends / parents will catch an aroma of rose and think of the green cardamom in your Napoli sauce, or dive into a bowl of white wine mussels and feel the missing piece of fresh curry leaf as a memory of you.

Showing multiple perspectives on spice usage helps to soften those really hard outlines of context that tie spices so strongly to Indian food. It enables you to appreciate this very old and very beautiful traditional food culture by working with the "everydayness" of spice in the way of an Indian, and finding something for yourself in that.

The Palate

What Is The Palate

No real good can come of using The Spice Companion without a little explanation about the working of your mouth: chiefly, the parts of the palate that I refer to throughout this book, and their roles in constructing flavour. I use this information to begin every spice class as it will make practical understanding of how spices work clearer. So for a couple of paragraphs I will lead you through key terminology relating to the mouth before diving into the broad topics of spice categories, fats, and—later—a detailed individual look at 57 different dried and fresh spices that I use on high rotation.

Why The Palate Matters
The "palate" refers to the interior mouth space. Your mouth is genius in its ability to multitask, and it's this ability that allows us to experience the various aromatic components contained within food as a mouthful of flavour. Your mouth multitasks by drawing aromatic information from the parts of the palate that are "signalling".

Each section of the palate signals a broadly general set of sensations. The mouth puts these sensations together and—voila—we have the experience of taste.

An important note: the complexity of the mouth means that more than one of the below references to "palate" takes in a part of the outer face or neck structure. The integration of our body systems and body parts means that it's difficult to isolate to just the interior of the mouth when discussing taste and flavour.

In no particular order of importance, these are the sections of the palate you will see referenced throughout the Companion.

Palate floor

The palate floor refers to the bottom of the mouth, ie the broad surface across the flat of the tongue. Bitter aromatics cause this part of the palate to signal. Information related from the palate floor gives the mouth the sensation of structure.

Mid palate

The mid palate refers to the horizontal middle of the tongue: if your forehead was north, and your chin was south, the mid palate would be your east-west indicator. Earth aromatics cause this part of the palate to signal. Information related from the mid palate relays information to the mouth about texture.

UPPER PALATE
The upper palate refers to the roof of the mouth. Hot aromatics cause this part of the palate to signal. Information related from the upper palate gives the mouth the sensation of height.

UPPER-MID PALATE
The upper-mid palate refers to the horizontal space beneath the roof of the mouth, in the space above the tongue. Forest floor aromatics cause this part of the palate to signal. Information related from the upper-mid palate provides the mouth with the sensation of movement.

BACK PALATE
The back palate refers to the back of the mouth, specifically the area of the back molars. Pungent aromatics cause this part of the palate to signal. Information related from the back palate provides a feeling of depth.

FRONT PALATE
The front palate refers to the front of the face, specifically the external area around the nose and the mouth. Warm aromatics cause this extension of the palate to signal. Information from the front palate provides the mouth with a sensation of rounded flavour.

Central palate
The central palate refers to the straight line from the bow of the lips to the back of the tongue. Acidic aromatics cause this part of the palate to signal. Information from the central palate offers the mouth the experience of clarity.

The gullet
The gullet refers to the internal throat from beneath the chin to the base of the collarbone. Astringent and sulphuric aromatics cause the gullet to signal. Information from the gullet provides the mouth with a feeling of spaciousness.

Cheeks
The cheek refers to the fleshy inner of the cheeks. Acidic aromatics cause this part of the palate to signal. Information from the inner cheek causes the mouth to experience the sensation of contraction.

Palate FAQs

1. *Do I need to put the spice in a particular spot in my mouth to feel and taste it properly?*
   No. The genius of the mouth is that it knows exactly what to do with what you give it.

2. *If I'm tasting spice on my own, how do I identify its taste?*

   This is a great question. You have to practice, keeping these two important questions in mind: when I put that spice in my mouth, which part of my mouth "signals" and what does that signal feel like? Do I feel it on my tongue? Does the sensation linger for a long time, or is it fleeting? Do I feel heat in my face? Is there a bitter or pungent quality that gets stuck in my molars, or along my jaw line? Does my mouth dry out, or become flooded with saliva? Noticing all of these aspects of the taste experience is how we build up our own internal "flavour library". It is a way of training ourselves to understand the information our mouth automatically gathers. Cross referencing your own experience against my descriptions of spice categories, and the individual descriptions of the spices themselves will help to form a life-long database that will—I hope—bring autonomy, creativity, and pleasure to your kitchen experiences.

Spice Categories

A World Beyond Recipe

When I first started teaching spice classes I had to find a way to break spice information into consumable bites. Using categories was an obvious solution. Use of aromatic categories is as old as cooking itself, and all cultures have their own language around classification. Western culinary culture counts on six tastes: salty, bitter, sweet, hot, acidic, and umami. Ayurvedic vocabulary has a different six: these are sour, pungent, astringent, sweet, salty, and bitter.

I've created 10 aromatic categories that take from both Eastern and Western taste traditions, and expand out from both. When it comes to spice most people consider aroma as the defining character. But beneath aroma each spice has a function. This is the bit about spice that I love to teach. Understanding the function of a spice is the gateway to being able to use aromatics with confidence in a free-form way. When you understand that *hot* category spices give the appearance of height and lightness to a dish, then you'll know to reach for a touch of ground red chilli or cayenne pepper if your meaty winter slow cook feels too heavy. If a new South East Asian recipe you're trying feels a little "too much" spice wise, then you can reach for a rounded sugar like a jaggery from your *sweet* category to smooth out and soften some of the intensity.

It's important to note that the form of a spice can alter its categorisation. This is because form has an impact on the way that we experience aroma. Form can also shift the functional impact of a spice. The best example of this is star anise. As a whole spice, **star anise** fits in the *structural* spice category. The seed of star anise, **aniseed**, fits in the *earth* spice category. **Aniseed powder** fits in the *warm* spice category.

Being even just a little bit familiar with spice categorisation will unlock a world of flavour beyond recipe. The categories below are listed alphabetically. Some of the language is known. Some of the vocabulary I've created to root the aromatic function of a particular spice group more firmly within the sensory space: *earth* spice, for example, explains not only the seedy, gritty and often soil-like flavour profiles of these spices, but also hints at this category's ability to anchor aroma to the palate.

All of these spice categories perform more than one function. I'll break down the most important, as they relate to use of this Spice Companion.

Cateogories are listed in alphabetical order.

Acidic Spice

CATEGORY OVERVIEW:
Acidic spices are some of the easiest to use free-form because they're so commonly eaten. Lemons. Limes. From a flavour perspective, acidic aroma is familiar to all and naturally delicious to the majority. From a functional perspective, the use of acidic spice facilitates two important roles.

In food, as in wine, structured lines of acidity provide guidance for the palate. Acidic spice provides a tight central palate line. This line is like a handrail that stops the mouth getting "lost" in the identification of complex or dense flavours.

Secondly, acidic spice stimulates the inner cheeks. Creating stimulation in this part of the palate causes the mouth to experience the sensation of puckering or contraction, which lends the illusion of "tighter" flavour for the whole dish.

Use acidic spices to fire up chilli, to provide a line of guidance through cloying warmth or sweetness, or to break open bitterness or smoke. A squeeze of lime or lemon juice over a dish with "brown" or unclear tones can delineate flavour and rescue the dish.

ACIDIC SPICE INCLUSIONS:
Tamarind. Amchur. Lemon. Lime. Sumac. Pomegranate molasses. Vinegars.

SPICE WITH ACIDIC ASPIRATIONS:
Fresh garlic. Raw onion.

Astringent-Sulphuric Spice

CATEGORY OVERVIEW:

The worth of *astringent-sulphuric* spices are in their sharp, nasal clearing impact. When they pierce the palate, these aromatics increase the mouth's ability to distinguish contrasts in dishes with complex flavour. A deeply held internal sweetness saves these spices from being brutish. Fresh astringent-sulphuric spice can be pleasant in the raw state.

ASTRINGENT-SULPHURIC SPICE INCLUSIONS:

Onion. Fresh garlic. Fresh ginger. Bay leaf. Indian bay leaf. Mustard seeds, black and yellow. Asafoetida.

SPICE WITH ASTRINGENT-SULPHURIC ASPIRATIONS:

Nutmeg powder. Clove buds. Clove powder. Mace powder. Mace flower. Kalonji.

Bitter Spice

CATEGORY OVERVIEW:
The dual roles of *bitter* spices are to provide structure and to induce the sensation of satiety—of repletion.

Structurally, bitterness is the spine of the aromatic world. A small amount of bitter spice in a dish will assist in holding the other aromatics upright. Strengthening the spine of a dish clarifies aromatic expression, particularly for simpler dishes that use fewer ingredients. In a classic Italian sugo, for example, the element of "time" in cooking is used to create structure. In a busy family, you could substitute time on the stove for a pinch of turmeric powder in that same sugo. This bitter addition will make the tomatoes appear richer, the basil more herbaceous, and give the black pepper deeper bite, without disturbing the sugo's classic flavour. The **bitterness** of turmeric has replaced **time** as the backbone for the dish.

Aromatically, the strong experience of bitter flavour curbs the appetite. A lack of bitter flavour in the diet leads to imbalanced cravings for sweets and a decrease in sensations of satiety—satiety can occur in the mouth before it occurs in the stomach. Strong flavours experienced orally signal pleasure, nourishment, and a sense of fullness.

BITTER SPICE INCLUSIONS:
Fenugreek seed. Fenugreek powder. Turmeric powder. Fresh turmeric.

SPICE WITH BITTER ASPIRATIONS:
Cumin powder. Mustard seeds, black and yellow.

Earth Spice

Category overview:
Earth spices are the grounding spices of the aromatic world. They are settling to the sensory body. Spices within this category share the function of providing mid palate weight and texture.

As a function, weight across the mid palate prevents companion aromatics from falling into a sinkhole: the mid palate is an important connection point between all areas of the mouth. Without earth spices drawing awareness to that space, a dish can easily lose dimension.

Texture helps with appetite control by ensuring the sensory body "feels" the process of eating, helping to accelerate feelings of fullness.

Earth spice inclusions:
Cumin powder. Cumin seed. Coriander powder. Fennel seed. Ajwain. Aniseed. Nigella seed.

Spice with earth aspirations:
Garam masala. Fennel powder. Aniseed powder.

Forest Floor Spice

CATEGORY OVERVIEW:
Forest floor spices are all about movement and that movement can be a gentle nudge or a quick shove, depending on the quantity of spice and whether they are fresh or dry. In a masala specifically, the way the spices move is a big part of the overall experience of pleasure. These forest floor spices can fan the fire of chilli or provide contrast to sulphuric aromatics.

FOREST FLOOR SPICE INCLUSIONS:
Curry leaf. Tulsi. Fenugreek leaf. Coriander leaf. Basil. Oregano. Parsley.

SPICE WITH FOREST FLOOR ASPIRATIONS:
Indian bay leaf. Bay leaf.

Hot Spice

CATEGORY OVERVIEW:
The category of *hot* spice draws flavour up and gives a masala its height. Take a moment to taste red ground chilli powder. Feel the burn as it sets fire to the tip of the tongue and flames the base of the throat. Concentrate and experience a lightening and illumination behind the eyes as if the top of the skull is lifted. That's chilli.

As chilli moves up and out through the roof of the palate, the bed of spice within the masala is pulled with it, elongating flavour.

Heat from peppercorn varietals is dirtier, earthy and lower in tonality. When roughly ground, peppers offer a textural experience. When finely ground, peppers have a persistent and resonant heat that builds around the molars. Combined, peppers and chillies create a jaw deep, high keynote that expands the mouthfeel and invites a fuller appreciation of the spice experience.

Hot spice inclusions:
Fresh red chilli. Fresh green chilli. Red chilli powder. Chilli flakes. Kashmiri chilli powder. Cayenne pepper. Paprika (all). Black pepper. Green pepper. White pepper. Szechuan pepper.

Spice with hot aspirations:
Onion. Fresh garlic. Fresh ginger. Ginger powder. Mustard seeds, black and yellow.

Structural Spice

CATEGORY OVERVIEW:
The category of *structural* spice takes in aromatics that are used in whole form and fulfil two distinct roles: to create exclamation points of flavour, and to strengthen the aromatic framework of a dish.

Structural spices do not blend. They are distinct, powerful, and require a longer slower cooking process to maximise their impact in the pan and the dish.

STRUCTURAL SPICE INCLUSIONS:
Cinnamon quills. Cassia bark. Star anise. Black cardamom. Green cardamom. Clove buds. Mace flower.

SPICE WITH STRUCTURAL ASPIRATIONS:
Turmeric powder. Fenugreek powder. Bay leaf. Indian bay leaf.

Sweet Spice

CATEGORY OVERVIEW:

The idea of *sweet* pertains more to sugars used alongside spices than a category of dried or fresh aromatics, but that sweet addition is an important contribution. A little bit of sugar used with spice rounds off hard edges and sharp contrasts resulting in a gentler aromatic experience. Subtle use of a sugar like jaggery alongside simplified spice blends is a traditional way to introduce children to more complex flavours and textures.

Jaggery (unrefined cane sugar) is the preferred sugar when creating an Indian masala. A more refined caster sugar is useful in Mediterranean-style dishes benefitting from a sharper sweet offset. In terms of impact on health, a little bit of sugar in a pan of spices, whole fats, and fresh produce fits with a natural system of eating.

Sweet spice inclusions:
Jaggery. Caster sugar. Raw cane sugar. Rapadura. Coconut sugar. Honey. Molasses.

Spice with sweet aspirations:
Pomegranate molasses. Cassia powder.

Warm Spice

CATEGORY OVERVIEW:
These are what I call "the grandma spices", the aromas that are most associated with matriarchal love. Pleasure is an integral part of eating and *warm* spice is responsible for a lot of that "yum" response to foods. The beauty of the warm category of aromatics is that like a wise matriarch guides you and helps you grow, these spices pave the way for more developed flavours.

WARM SPICE INCLUSIONS:
Cinnamon powder. Cassia powder. Ginger powder. Cardamom powder. Mace powder. Garam masala. Nutmeg powder. Clove powder. Fennel powder. Aniseed powder.

SPICE WITH WARM ASPIRATIONS:
Clove bud. Star anise. Jaggery.

Salt

CATEGORY OVERVIEW:
Salt isn't technically a spice, but for those of us in love with aromatics and their magic, its contribution is critical and defining.

One of salt's defining roles is to help create clear aromatic communication. Salt does this by increasing the volume of spice tonality. Salt makes flavour louder and clearer. Better enunciated flavour is easier for the mouth to "hear". And the easier it is for the palate to define an aromatic structure, the more delicious the entire mouthful will be.

As the complexity of the spice structure increases, so does the importance of salt.

SALT INCLUSIONS:
Fine pink salt. White lake salt. White sea salt. Fleur de sel. Smoked salt. Indian black salt.

SPICE WITH SALT ASPIRATIONS:
Sumac. Lime. Onion. Asafoetida.

Fats

Flavour Influencers

FATS ARE THE FIRST INGREDIENT I consider when thinking about a dish. This is because fats have so much influence over spice expression: they work as filters on spice.

Think of the ingredients in your dish like a photo. You can use a photo filter to draw attention to or away from things in the photo. You can sharpen or soften lines and intensify shadows or brighten dark corners. The fats you chose in a dish are like those filters, creating an overlay that can deepen, sharpen, sweeten, or harden the aromatic experience.

Photo filters are a creative tool that help you use a photo to tell a specific story. In cooking, fats are used much the same way. They help you tell a specific and personal spice story when you cook.

Coconut Oil

PROFILE:
The fragrant character of coconut oil frames masala in a joyous light. It is cool and slick; it lingers on the palate; and it soothes the systems of the body. Spice students who don't love its coconut flavour will tell me they prefer not to use this fat, that they find its aroma overpowering. But for me, coconut oil is less about translating a "coconut" taste than it is wrapping the mouth in brightness.

Spice responds to coconut oil with openness and generosity. As a fat, it draws forward sweetness, light, and acidity in spice and these are all points of pleasure for the palate. This fat is a natural inclusion in the street food-style salads and vibrant seafood dishes found in Vietnamese and Thai cooking. When I want to make a dish where the result is festive and high toned, coconut oil is my go-to fat.

USE IT WHEN:
Coconut oil will lift a dark, flat masala by raising the appearance of sweetness and acidity. Use it when you've been heavy-handed with *earth* spice, or when you want to carry more heat and acidity through less textural produce such as skinless, boneless chicken or leaner and cheaper beef cuts that have heavier fibrous tissue and less fat.

AYURVEDA:
Coconut oil cools excess heat and inflammation in the body. It nourishes the nervous system and boosts energy and thyroid function.

COMPANION FATS:
Coconut oil will heighten the "hot" quality of mustard oil, lighten ghee's rich mouthfeel, and shift sesame oil into a heavier and warmer gear.

ENHANCE COCONUT OIL WITH:
Clove buds. Cracked black pepper. Cumin seed. Fennel seed. Green cardamom. Star anise.

SOFTEN COCONUT OIL WITH:
Cassia powder. Cinnamon powder. Cumin powder. Turmeric powder.

Ghee

PROFILE:
The mother fat of India, ghee is buttery, dense, sweet, and floury. Ghee coats the mouth with a long-lasting thick texture that carries flavour and provides a reliable platform for complex aromatic structures.

Ghee is a balanced fat. It spreads evenly across the palate, resulting in balanced, classical spice expression. Ghee draws forward the true character of each singular spice with clarity. With ghee, chillies are hot, floral, and sweet; cumin seeds are warm pine and menthol; cinnamon quill is wooded, sugared, and tall; and turmeric powder is gingered, bitter, and oily.

In the spice tempering process, ghee ensures a clarity of expression that results in very defined aromatic blends.

USE IT WHEN:
Many traditional regional Indian dishes derive their base aromatic character from ghee. Use it when making a dal

tadka or when tempering masala. When cooking Italian, Spanish, or Mexican foods ghee can be combined with olive oil to soften fresh aromatics. At breakfast time pair ghee with olive oil when cooking eggs to achieve a richer result.

Ayurveda:
Ghee is a sattvic food. In Ayurveda, it is considered sweet, cold, and heavy. It is a fat to support internal balance for all body types across all seasons.

Spoken of in India's ancient Vedic texts—the philosophical texts that form the basis of Hinduism—ghee is used in temple rituals and as the fuel for candles during faith festivities.

Companion fats:
Used in combination, mustard oil will sharpen ghee's sweetness. Sesame oil will lift ghee's weight. Coconut oil will excite and sharpen ghee's softer quality.

Enhance ghee with:
Ajwain. Dried fenugreek leaf. Tamarind.

Soften ghee with:
Turmeric powder. Cumin seed. Ginger powder. Cinnamon quill. Cassia bark. Sesame seed.

Macadamia Oil

PROFILE:
Broad and sweet, very slightly bitter and mild, macadamia oil has an unctuous mouthfeel akin to ghee. It is slippery and without edge. Much of its aroma is recessed by the oily quality of the fat but this can be drawn forward by intelligent use of spice and companion fats.

Macadamia oil is a valuable vegan replacement for ghee: the broad, slightly sweet, and relatively neutral profile—along with its round mouthfeel—makes it comparatively similar. As a filter on spice, it rounds out the edges of *acidic* spice, smooths the gritty texture of *earth* spice, and thins *warm* and *bitter* spice.

Macadamia oil tends to flatten flavour, so I rarely recommend using it on its own. If cooking vegan, pair with companion fats (see below) to lift the dish.

USE IT WHEN:
Cooking without dairy so as a vegan replacement for ghee with any vegetable sabzi.

Companion fats:
Macadamia oil doesn't give as much back to the end dish as ghee does, which means using it alongside a more vibrant or aggressive fat will help to ensure that the total flavour profile of the spice blend is not too muted.

Sesame oil draws forward macadamia's nutty quality. Mustard oil lifts and brightens its dense, buttery weight.

Enhance macadamia oil with:
Ajwain. Cumin seed. Cassia powder. Star anise. Dried red chilli powder. Clove bud. Garam masala. Fenugreek powder. Tamarind.

Soften macadamia oil with:
Coriander powder. Turmeric powder. Jaggery. Ginger powder.

Mustard Oil

Profile:
Largely unknown to Western home cooks, the hot and pungent aroma of mustard oil brings to mind wasabi, fresh horseradish, or hot English mustard. The hidden floral body of mustard oil steps forward when it is tasted raw.

Viscous and sharp, mustard oil creates a long-lasting seal for the palate which is ideal for supporting complex spice. This fat draws forward the pungent, hot, floral, and shadowed character of all spice. Mustard oil makes chilli sizzle and *earth* spice glitter. It strengthens and blunts *warm* and *sweet* aromatics.

Use it when:
The aromatic punch and rich viscosity of mustard oil makes it a powerful flavour enhancer. Use it when browning lamb shanks, or prepping bone-in chicken cuts for slow cooks. Replace olive oil or vegetable oil with

mustard oil when making a base for meat and vegetable curries. Try preparing Mexican food with a blend of mustard oil and olive oil to increase the pungency of oregano, cayenne, and cumin powder.

Ayurveda:
Considered a detoxifier, mustard oil is said to have anti-aging properties as well as being an antioxidant. Ayurveda practitioners believe that the vitamin E in mustard oil increases immunity and improves circulation. Its heat does lend it an inflammatory quality, so use less if ageing or when suffering inflammatory conditions.

Companion fats:
Pair ghee with mustard oil to soften the oil's intensity. Coconut oil will raise mustard oil's tonality. Sesame oil will increase mustard oil's heat and pungency. Peanut oil will thin its viscosity.

Enhance mustard oil with:
Black mustard seed. Yellow mustard seed. Garlic. Onion. Fresh ginger.

Soften mustard oil with:
Fresh curry leaf. Coriander powder. Mace powder. Jaggery. Cassia powder.

Olive Oil

PROFILE:
Olive oil has multiple flavour profiles since it is produced from different types of olives. It can be peppery and biting, grassy and herbaceous, green and mild, or any combination thereof. Regardless of flavour, olive oil has a uniform consistency: slightly more viscous than other vegetable oils but thinner than mustard and nut oils.

Olive oil thins complex spice structure and draws forward peppery, pungent, and grassy characters in aromatics. Ideally, match olive oil with pungent fresh spices showing wet and penetrative aromas with *forest floor* category spices to create turbulent motion that imbues the oil with more texture and interest.

USE IT WHEN:
Olive oil draws out bitterness in dried spice, so I don't recommend its use with Indian cuisine. There is one specific exception: when matching traditional Indian meat

dishes with tannic and gripping red wines such as Cabernet Sauvignon that find companionship in olive oil's bay leaf character.

For the most part I use olive oil when making Mediterranean or Middle Eastern recipes.

Companion fats:
Pair olive oil with butter to approximate ghee. Mustard oil will increase the peppered heat of olive oil. Peanut oil will provide olive oil with increased aromatic texture. Coconut oil with make it creamier.

Enhance olive oil with:
Fresh galangal. Onion. Garlic. Basil. Black pepper. Oregano. Bay leaf.

Soften olive oil with:
Kashmiri chilli. Jaggery. White pepper. Tomatoes.

Peanut Oil

PROFILE:
Peanut oil is nutty yet neutral and sits in the centre of the mouth. It has a mild taste and a light feel on the palate. Thinner than mustard oil, it is more viscous and textured than olive oil.

This oil is used in Central and South East Asian cuisines as it is ideal for high heat cooking: peanut oil is capable of carrying vibrant, fresh spice aromas, and makes an excellent base for the salty, umami-laden, liquid condiments common to recipes from these regions.

Peanut oil flattens the flavours of dried spice when tempered at low heat. Counteract this character by using it in combination with a brighter fat.

USE IT WHEN:
I think of peanut oil as the perfect wok accompaniment. Use it when frying fresh spice at high heat with liquid condiments like soy sauce, rice wines, or fish sauce. Try

it when frying pakoras or samosas in combination with mustard oil to increase the crispiness of the pastry.

Companion fats:
Combine peanut oil with mustard oil for an aromatic combination when frying at higher temperatures.

Enhance peanut oil with:
Fresh red chilli. Fresh green chilli. Onion. Garlic. Fresh ginger. Fresh galangal. Tamarind. Curry leaf.

Soften peanut oil with:
Fenugreek powder. Turmeric powder. Coriander powder. Jaggery. Garam masala. Black cardamom. Cinnamon quill. Cassia bark.

Sesame Oil

PROFILE:
When used as a finishing touch, sesame oil is perceived by the mouth as warm and thick, lending a unique, nutty lift. Its viscosity and distinct aromatic profile make it an interesting oil to use with broader oils such as coconut, macadamia, and ghee that can carry its flavour.

Sesame oil draws out astringent notes in *warm* spice, heats *acidic* spice, and emphasises the grounded quality of *earth* spice while making them more forward and pungent. It also stimulates *hot* spice.

Sesame oil can be used at high heat if paired with a high heat oil.

USE IT WHEN:
It only takes a touch of sesame oil to make an impact. Use it when cooking with mustard oil to increase nutty and hot characters in a dish. Liven up earthy dishes by drizzling it as a finishing oil; as an example, a touch of sesame oil in a molé sauce adds an elegant end polish.

COMPANION FATS:
Combine sesame oil with peanut oil, mustard oil, or vegetable oil for an aromatic combination when frying at higher temperatures. For lower temperature cooking, sesame oil is exceptional when married with a broader aromatic oil such as a coconut, ghee, or macadamia oil. These combinations carry forward its flavour with beauty.

ENHANCE SESAME OIL WITH:
Spring onions. Fresh ginger. Fresh lime. Szechuan pepper. White lake salt.

SOFTEN SESAME OIL WITH:
Fine pink salt. Honey. Cashew paste. Coconut milk. Fresh coconut.

Yoghurt

Profile:
Thick, creamy, cool, and acidic, natural yoghurt is a beautiful fat with which to bed down spice.

Technically not a frying fat, yoghurt is traditionally used across many regions of India to marinate and brown meats. Its rich and dense dairy weight creates a buffer between spice and the palate, softening the experience of taste.

Yoghurt softens *earth* and *bitter* spice, further articulates *acidic* and *astringent-sulphuric* spice, mellows *hot* spice, and freshens *forest floor* spice.

Use it when:
I use an extraordinary amount of yoghurt in my kitchen because of the way it tenderises meat and softens spice. Use it when browning lamb alongside mustard oil to keep the meat tender. Make it a base when marinating boneless, skinless chicken with spice before cooking.

(This embeds flavour into the chicken for more depth and impact. Otherwise, boneless, skinless chicken protein tends to "slip" beneath flavour, resulting in a bland dish.)

AYURVEDA:
In Ayurvedic medicine, yoghurt is an "occasional" food that should not be consumed in quantity because of its cold and heavy quality. The preferred yoghurt in Ayurveda is *dahi*, a fermented yoghurt commonly made in Indian households.

COMPANION FATS:
Yoghurt works well across the entire fat spectrum. It preserves the heat of mustard oil while simultaneously clarifying its recessed floral qualities. Kashmiri cooking pairs yoghurt with ghee for added richness.

ENHANCE YOGHURT WITH:
Sumac. Amchur. Pomegranate molasses. Fresh lime. Tamarind. Refined sugars. Whole bay leaf. Vinegars. Nutmeg powder. Clove buds. Onion. Garlic. Tomatoes.

SOFTEN YOGHURT WITH:
Garam masala. Turmeric powder. Star anise. Cinnamon powder. Cinnamon quill. Black cardamom. Green cardamom. Fennel powder.

* A Note On

Butter:
Butter browns and caramelises at low heat, changing the profile of tempered spice and proving itself too light to support complex aromatic blends. Butter is most useful to mellow strong oils and pungent fats, or to add texture and weight to thin or "slippery" oils.

Lard:
Lard isn't useful enough in spice cooking to warrant a section. However reserved fat from roasted meats can be a great base for a soft masala blend. Use this lard-masala blend to cook leftover greens like wilted lettuce or sad broccoli for a delicious no-waste side dish.

Vegetable oils:
Vegetable oils are commonly used for higher temperature cooking or frying. As utilitarian oils, they do not express any primary flavours and are not useful when building aromatic structure other than to use a small quantity to "undo" a masala that has become too tight or complex. The exception is the use of cold pressed vegetable oils that retain their viscosity and flavour: though rare, some producers are beginning to revive the reputation of blighted vegetable oils by using non GM crops and considering the processing with integrity.

Spices

Spice Terminology

BEFORE WE DIVE HEADLONG INTO working with individual spices I thought it might be worth detailing a little of the terminology that you'll see recur throughout the descriptions. Chiefly what I'm referring to when I talk about **primary**, **secondary**, and **tertiary** characters in singular aromatics, along with frequent references to **aroma**, **texture**, and **shape**.

Spices are inherently complex, which is what makes them so fun to use. Breaking down taste information into a few distinct components is the best way to translate the experience of taste. And an understanding of how to taste spice is of key importance when it comes to using spice.

SPICE USAGE:
Spices are like people: they work better together. Think about salt and pepper: salt drives flavour, and pepper anchors it—together they pack a more textural aromatic

punch. All Indian regional cuisine derives its character from ways of blending spice that speak to cultural, geographic, social, and faith traditions. But it doesn't always have to be so roots-deep. Understanding a little bit about spice character makes it easier to combine aromatics. Understanding that **turmeric powder** has primary characters of **ginger**, and secondary characters of **bitter orange rind** means I might start to consider turmeric powder as an ingredient in my **orange cake**, for example. I read a lot about "intuitive cooking". I agree that it's a brilliant way to cook. But there needs to be a pretty deep understanding of the inherent aromatic experience of a spice, fat, or produce before the practice of intuitive cooking feels accessible. I hope this pre-spice breakdown will help you to further utilise the information on individual spices contained within the pages following these.

PRIMARY CHARACTER:
The primary character of a spice is the flavour or flavours that hit the tongue in the first instance. The primary characters are the most known. Cooks with only minimal spice knowledge will generally understand that fennel seed is **liquorice**, that cumin powder is **soil-like**, and that turmeric powder appears as **bitter** and **gingery**. This aspect of spice is your broad brushstroke guide in terms of possible usage, taste, and the aromatic contribution a spice will make to a dish.

SECONDARY CHARACTER:
The secondary characters of a spice are the pieces of aromatic information that follow once the initial primary tastes have expressed. This aromatic information requires more focus to identify, but is not too difficult when following taste prompts like the ones given in my Companion. Understanding secondary characters in spices helps us to understand the ways in which a spice can be transformed by spice blending. It might not seem obvious to use **fenugreek powder** with **green cardamom pods**, but once you understand that green cardamom pods have primary characters of **mint** and **rose**, and fenugreek powder has primary character of **appleseed** and a secondary character of **mint**, then the aromatic alignment becomes a little more obvious—apple, mint, and rose sound like a pretty well matched triplicate of aromas. But even if you're very new to spices and this kind of thinking seems way too sophisticated, rest assured understanding the secondary character of spices will still be a huge help: when we fail with new experiments in flavour, it's good to know the full aromatic story of the spices with which we failed. This helps us to ascertain where we went wrong.

TERTIARY CHARACTER:
Not every spice has tertiary character. "Lighter" spices tend to seem primary and secondary only. Even in complex spices, tertiary character refers more to a **feel in the**

mouth than an actual **aroma**. The next three explanations below will help to explain the difference between shape, aroma, and texture.

Aroma:
Aroma is the aspect of spices with which most people are most familiar. Aroma is obvious: the smell of **roses** is **floral**. Floral is the description of the aroma. **Ginger powder** has a **gingery** aroma. **Cassia powder** has an aroma of **sugared-cinnamon**. Aroma essentially refers to both smell and primary character. Aroma is a fundamental way to understand spice and will offer a first insight into which category a spice belongs. *Earth* spices have an earth aroma. *Forest floor* spices are generally herbaceous. *Hot* category spices have an aroma of heat. *Warm* spices generally smell quite sweet. You get the picture. Though aroma is only the beginning of the spice story, it remains a fairly strong indicator of what the general aromatic contribution of that spice will be.

Texture:
Texture is the aspect of spices that refers to the **mouthfeel** of the spice. Mouthfeel is quite literally the feel of an edible ingredient in the mouth. **Cumin seed** feels **desiccated** and **dry**, for example. **Fenugreek powder** is **gluey** and sets like concrete to the roof of the mouth and the backs of the front teeth. Texture impacts our experience of taste because the texture of a spice impacts our experience of flavour. The **wet** nature of **fresh ginger**

makes that form of the spice **astringent** and **sharp**. The **dried** nature of **ginger powder** makes that form of the spice **round** and **hot**. This is true of all foods. Consider how chocolate when melted becomes immediately richer. Paying attention to texture will help you to understand how to combine **contrasting** spices: if you have a lot of powdery spices in a dish, understand that utilising a spice with a contrasting texture—a seedy *earth* spice or an herbaceous fresh leaf spice—will create interest and dimension.

SHAPE:
Perhaps the most esoteric of spice descriptors, **shape** refers to the structural feel of a spice in the mouth. Shape is different to texture. Texture is quite literally the feel of the spice. Shape refers to the effect the spice has on the interior of the mouth. *Acidic* spices like **sumac** and **tamarind** create that cheek puckering feeling of **contraction**. An obvious spice like **cassia powder** creates a sensation of **fullness**. **Dried fenugreek leaf** acts as you imagine a *forest floor* spice would: it rustles around, creating a distinct feeling of **movement**. The shape of a spice is helpful once we become sophisticated enough in our spice thinking to consider the construction of architecture in a dish. For a beginner, just recognising the sensation of shape in spices where it is obvious (those aforementioned acidic spices) is information to file away and build upon when ready.

Ajwain

CATEGORY:
Earth spice.

PROFILE:
Ajwain seed is a pungent spice with a distinctive triplicate of primary aromas that segue from **eucalyptus** through **soap** and into **kerosene**. It leaves a residual taste of "garage floor" in the mouth that receives mixed reactions from most of my spice students. Secondary aromatic notes include **bitter celery** and **thyme**.

FORM:
A small, dried seed that that has a thin tail. Its seed pod is ridged. Its colour is bronze khaki. Ajwain resembles aniseed in colour and shape, though ajwain is smaller when the two are compared side by side.

IN COOKING:
Ajwain is an exotic spice you should get to know. Traditionally used in Indian fried breads such as pooris, paranthas, and besan flour-based fried snacks, ajwain adds a sharp and cutting flavour to fried dough. Try adding to a Kashmiri bitter gourd and yoghurt sabzi or add to the glass rim of a Bloody Mary for an unusual dimension to a cocktail. Ajwain's very pungent and distinct aroma makes it useful as an addition to any dish that requires sharpening: think about a slow cooked pork dish or an eggplant moussaka with a rich tomato and béchamel sauce. Ajwain seed would make an interesting addition to homemade sausages. It's also an excellent digestive spice, making it a great addition to your kitchen spice rotation.

QUANTITY:
One-half teaspoon is sufficient in dishes feeding four to six people.

USE WITH:
White salt. Fresh chilli. Fresh turmeric. Fenugreek powder. Fennel seed.

REPLACE WITH:
Caraway seed.

ALSO CALLED:
Carom. Bishop's weed.

Amchur

Category:
Acidic spice.

Profile:
Amchur is ground from dried green mangoes and has a delicious aromatic body redolent of **sweet lime** and **sherbert**. It has secondary notes of **flat cola**, and a very subtle herbaceous quality akin to **coriander seed**. Amchur exhibits a **soft acidity**.

Form:
A dried powder with a dense texture akin to partially wet sand.

In cooking:
If you love lime, you'll love amchur. Widely used in North Indian cuisine, amchur is commonly found in Kashmiri cooking. As an *acidic* spice, amchur shoots light through

pungent and dense masala. One of its key qualities is persistence: amchur maintains its character through heat and cooking time. Amchur has a gentler impact than lemon or lime so can be ideal for use with seafood. Traditionally amchur is used in chaat masala, as a protein tenderiser in marinades, and to add delicate acidity to classic Kashmiri dishes. Unlike many dried and ground spices, amchur is delicious when used raw. Consider sprinkling a little with salt and chilli onto fresh mango. Use amchur as a seasoning on roast lamb or roast vegetables alongside salt and pepper; use it in a tagine or slow cook for a hint of acidity.

QUANTITY:
One-third to one teaspoon in dishes feeding four to six people.

USE WITH:
Cinnamon quills. Fresh curry leaf. Black pepper. Kashmiri chilli. Ginger powder. Turmeric powder. Fine pink salt.

REPLACE WITH:
Sumac.

ALSO CALLED:
Dried green mango powder.

Aniseed

CATEGORY:
Earth spice.

PROFILE:
Though they do serve as each other's replacement, aniseed and fennel seed do not share the same aromatic profile. Aniseed has a dark **Dutch liquorice** quality that has primary notes of **salt** and a higher octave of **sweetness**. It is **chewy** in texture with a **strong aroma** and a **recessed bitterness**.

FORM:
A petite dried seed that is ribbed and has a very thin tail. It is silvered khaki in colour and can be confused with ajwain seed, though aniseed is slightly larger.

IN COOKING:
Liquorice lovers pay attention. Aniseed is a pushy, dominating spice and the intense, chewy texture lingers. With

a heavy protein like beef, aniseed contributes strong sweetness. Its profile is well suited to pickling, and can be used to liven up earthy vegetables like beetroot, swede, and parsnip. When used sparingly, it's lovely with chicken and fish.

QUANTITY:
One-half teaspoon is sufficient in dishes feeding four to six people.

USE WITH:
Fennel seed. Ajwain. Jaggery. Fresh coriander leaf. Red chilli. Cassia powder. Fine pink salt.

REPLACE WITH:
Fennel seed.

ALSO CALLED:
Saunf. Anise. Sweet cumin.

Aniseed Powder

Category:
Warm spice.

Profile:
Changing the form of aniseed affects its aroma enormously. Grinding down the husk of the aniseed releases more **soil-like** qualities through aniseed powder resulting in **tempered liquorice** and **moist hay** characters. The **Dutch liquorice salt** becomes a secondary or recessed experience.

Form:
Concrete sand in texture, it is fluffy but heavier than green cardamom or coriander powder. The colour is that of dark sand.

In cooking:
Aniseed powder is much milder and simpler to use than aniseed. In traditional Kashmiri Pandit cooking, aniseed

powder is like a key to the golden gateway: a spice used virtually daily alongside ginger powder, cloves, cinnamon quills, and garam masala. Fennel powder as a *warm* spice is an important component of pleasure. It fills the front palate with pretty aromas that whet the appetite. But aniseed powder has darker qualities, like recessed salt and a hot pungency. Use aniseed powder in dishes of fried potato with salt to create a bit more "shape" and interest. (Potato—unless it is particularly well grown—can be quite bland.) Aniseed powder marries well with pork and can be used to rub into the pork skin with salt to make an extra tasty crackling. With ocean fish, aniseed powder draws forward the saline quality while also touching on any sweet characters within the flesh.

Quantity:
One-half to two teaspoons in dishes feeding four to six people.

Use with:
Fennel seed. Mace powder. Sumac. Cumin powder. Garam Masala. Black cardamom. Ginger powder.

Replace with:
Equal parts fennel powder and green cardamom powder.

Also called:
Saunf powder.

Asafoetida

CATEGORY:
Astringent-sulphuric spice.

PROFILE:
Asafoetida is used in Kashmiri Pandit cooking as a garlic and onion substitute. It has a very strong aroma reminiscent of **pineapple**, **onion** and **blue cheese**. The liquid form is milder than the powdered form.

FORM:
As a resin, asafoetida looks like putty when very fresh. As it ages, the putty form dries into a darker, firmer form the colour and texture of Scottish tablet. As a powder, asafoetida is a very fine, buttercup yellow.

IN COOKING:
For lots of Western cooks asafoetida seems like a bit of a mystery, but think of it as a garlic and onion replacement.

This is how we use it in traditional Pandit cooking. The use of asafoetida as a garlic and onion replacement in Kashmiri Pandit cooking has its origin in spiritual practice. These two vegetables are said to be "impure" or heating to the body system therefore disturbing internal balance and spiritual focus. But sulphuric elements like onion and garlic are important to masala blends. So, asafoetida to the rescue! The confronting smell of the dried powder (the resin is aromatically softer) transforms into a sweet oniony aroma and taste once tempered.

As a dried powder, asafoetida is added to the base of the pan. As a resin dissolved in water, it can be added throughout cooking as dictated by taste and recipe instruction. Like all astringent-sulphuric spices, it thins out dense flavours and provides more space within which aromas can be expressed. I think it's indispensable in red meat slow cooks in wintertime.

Quantity:
A pinch to one-third of a teaspoon of the powder in dishes feeding four to six people. The resin water is applied in drops throughout the cooking process, using no more than one teaspoon in total in dishes feeding four to six people.

Use with:
Cinnamon quills. Fine pink salt. Kashmiri red chilli. Whole garam masala. Fresh ginger.

REPLACE WITH:
Garlic and onion together.

ALSO CALLED:
Hing.

Bay Leaf

Category:
Forest floor spice.

Profile:
The leaf of the bay laurel tree can be used either fresh or dried. In the dried form, the leaf imparts a definitively **bitter** and **sharp** flavour. The profile is distinctly **herbaceous** with notes of **oregano** and **thyme** wrapping around a **pungent leaf bite**. Secondary notes approach **eucalyptus**.

Form:
A very dark green, glossy, classically shaped leaf that dulls to khaki when dried. From the bay laurel tree.

In cooking:
We all frequently use bay leaf, but few of us understand why. Essentially bay leaf adds savoury texture and a gentle

astringent quality to food. "Astringent" refers to an aroma that's nasal clearing: think of the impact of raw onion. But bay leaf is much gentler. One or two dried leaves in a classic mirepoix or soffritto will add fresh aromatic dimension. Similarly the addition of dried bay leaf to cream based sauces is a soft way to contribute savoury texture. Dried bay leaf forms part of garam masala and is used in Kashmiri mutton and chicken dishes, often in the meat browning process. This texture is a contrast to the rich umami character created by browning. Try fresh bay leaf in panna cotta with lavender or honey.

QUANTITY:
One to three leaves in dishes feeding four to six people.

USE WITH:
Star anise. Paprika smoked. Nutmeg powder. Clove powder.

REPLACE WITH:
Equal parts cumin powder and dried thyme.

ALSO CALLED:
Tej patta.

Indian Bay Leaf

CATEGORY:
Forest floor spice.

PROFILE:
With a more floral expression than the common bay leaf, Indian bay leaf has primary notes of **potpourri** dominated by **pink rose** and **musk**. Secondary notes fall into the realm of the familiar herbaceous **bay aromas** with a whisper of **eucalypt**.

FORM:
A very dark green, glossy, classically shaped leaf that dulls to khaki when dried. From the bay laurel tree, it looks almost identical to the classic bay leaf. The difference between the two is aromatic.

IN COOKING:
Its inherent character of floral rose and musk makes Indian bay leaf a less strident element than bay leaf when

used in a masala. Indian bay leaf veers toward cloying when paired with similarly floral spices like green cardamom and dried oregano, but it is complemented by warmth, fat, and heat. Use Indian bay leaf in rogan josh to impart a hint of sweet rose garden in a dish rich with savoury umami flavour. Indian bay leaf contrasts the sweetness of pork ribs and provides an interesting spice tangent for bitter greens. Though Indian bay leaf and common bay leaf have quite different flavour profiles, they perform the same function of moving flavour from the base of the mouth and spreading aroma into the hard-to-reach upper-mid palate.

QUANTITY:
One to three leaves in dishes feeding four to six people.

USE WITH:
Cinnamon powder. Ginger powder. Ghee. Jaggery. Nigella seed. Fine white pepper.

REPLACE WITH:
Equal parts green cardamom pods and dried oregano.

ALSO CALLED:
Tej patta.

Cardamom Black

CATEGORY:
Structural spice.

PROFILE:
Primary aromas of **smoke** and **char** with companion tones of **camphor** and **warm resin**. A secondary character of **mint** relates black cardamom back to its close spice playmate of green cardamom.

FORM:
A wizened pod of brown-black colour like a faded sepia print. The pods vary from "pistachio" through to "small stone fruit pip" in size.

IN COOKING:
A member of the ginger family and a cousin to green cardamom, this is a sexy spice. A single pod with the husk cracked is enough to pack a powerful aromatic punch.

The smoke of black cardamom will wind seductively around chilli and *acidic* spice bringing a warm, dark, and shadowy texture and depth to any dish. Its smoky characteristic means this intense spice can be softened by soft fats and *warm* category spices. Try a single black cardamom in a tomato soup with cream and black pepper. A few pods in a sugo bring depth to spaghetti Bolognese. Use black cardamom with rich cheese sauces to darken and texture the sweet dairy density. Classically, try it in gobi sabzi to draw out the latent shadow and elegance of cauliflower.

QUANTITY:
Two to three pods in dishes feeding four to six people.

USE WITH:
Cinnamon powder or quill. Amchur. Dried ground chilli. Clove buds. Bay leaves. Sumac. Black pepper.

REPLACE WITH:
A combination of bay leaf and clove powder.

ALSO CALLED:
Badi elaichi. Bengal cardamom. Brown cardamom. Indian cardamom. Greater cardamom.

Cardamom Green

Category:
Structural spice.

Profile:
Green cardamom has primary aromatic characters of **rose husk** through to **mint** and **spring eucalypt**. Secondary characters of **black pepper**, **camphor**, and **warm resin** are evidence of its close ties to black cardamom. Green cardamom is aromatically very complex, making it a spice to use sparingly.

Form:
Faded pistachio-green pods with a hessian textural quality that are shaped like an over-sized pine nut.

In cooking:
The distinct strength and very floral husk of green cardamom makes it a spice prone to aromatic mishap in

over-enthusiastic hands: too much of this single spice in a dish will consume subtler tastes. As a *structural* spice, green cardamom releases over time through the produce and so its overuse is difficult to correct. Err on the side of caution. Green cardamom pods work well with savoury foods that have very strong and driving flavour—dishes that are distinct. I love to use this spice in a chicken cacciatore heavy with tomato, olive, and caper. Green cardamom add contrast to richly sticky soy and oyster sauce-driven beef cheek. It is a natural marriage with carrot in traditional Indian savoury (gajar sabzi) or sweet (gajar halwa) dishes. And green cardamom is always a good idea with dairy-based desserts.

QUANTITY:
Two to three pods in dishes feeding four to six people.

USE WITH:
Mace powder. Kala namak. Black cardamom. Amchur. Kashmiri chilli. Tamarind. Coconut milk.

REPLACE WITH:
Equal parts Indian bay leaf and star anise.

ALSO CALLED:
Elaichi.

Cardamom Green Powder

CATEGORY:
Warm spice.

PROFILE:
Green cardamom powder is sweet with an aroma of **rose honey** and **toasted almond** atop the quality of **saffron cedar**. Unusually for a powder, it retains almost as much character as the whole spice. Secondary aromas are **musk** and **mint** in a nod to its pod form.

FORM:
A powder in two textures: the flossy and pollen-like bulk of this ground spice is akin to coriander powder, flecked with fine pieces of the pod's husk. It is khaki in colour with a pale green blush.

In cooking:
As a powder, green cardamom is less intense than when used in the whole form. It brings warmth to savoury and sweet dishes while still giving depth with its contrast of mint and cedar against fragrant rose. Like garam masala, you can add it at the end of a dish for extra complexity. It is beautiful when stirred through a dish of slow-cooked lamb. Green cardamom powder draws forward the savoury quality of pumpkin while giving depth to the vegetable's sweetness: try a little to finish a pumpkin soup. Just a pinch of green cardamom alongside cassia powder and honey will add a savoury sweetness to a morning bowl of porridge. The smallest amount of cardamom powder can match with rose water and white pepper to bring a bit of spice to a classic pavlova recipe.

Quantity:
One-third to one teaspoon in dishes feeding four to six people.

Use with:
Fine white pepper. Garam masala. Green cardamom pods. Star anise. Nutmeg powder. Honey. Almonds.

REPLACE WITH:
A combination of saffron and coriander powder.

ALSO CALLED:
Elaichi powder.

Cassia Bark

Category:
Structural spice.

Profile:
Cassia cinnamon is a cousin of true cinnamon, though with a stronger and rounder profile suited for use with spice in the *hot* and *acidic* categories. Cassia bark is **woody**, **pungent**, and **hot**. The **sweet-sugared** notes of cassia powder are recessed deep inside the structural form of this whole spice. The bark is much **rougher** and **darker** than the fine elegance of the cinnamon quill.

Form:
Rough and open bark which is a rich, dark tan in colour.

In cooking:
Getting to know cassia bark starts with the visual: comparing it with cinnamon quill is really instructive in

terms of understanding the impact cassia bark has on a dish. Whereas whole cinnamon is tight and refined, cassia bark is rougher, darker, more open and "obvious" in form. In the pan, cassia bark has a lot more aromatic push. It is hotter, more pungent, more obviously wooded, and sweeter than the cinnamon quill. The fact that it's not as delicate also means the bark can take a higher heat point. This makes cassia bark ideal for use in Chinese-Malay-style cuisines where high heat cooking of oyster sauce, fish sauce, and strong and fresh aromatics like hot chillies, galangal, ginger, and lemongrass dominate. Cassia bark is a powerful addition to pho stock, and in any slow-cooked ragu where fresh tomatoes star. Dad made a traditional kaddu sabzi (spiced pumpkin) with cassia bark, Kashmiri chilli powder, and mace flower that was so spicy and delicious that my second son as a toddler would cry in an agony-ecstasy of too-hot-won't-stop when eating it. Cassia bark and green cardamom make a powerfully warming chai.

Quantity:
One piece of bark in dishes feeding four to six people.

Use with:
Cinnamon quills. Turmeric powder. Curry leaf. Coriander leaf. Pomegranate molasses. Indian black salt. Fine white pepper.

REPLACE WITH:
A combination of cinnamon quill and clove buds.

ALSO CALLED:
Jangli dalchini. Chinese cinnamon. Poor man's cinnamon.

Cassia Powder

Category:
Warm spice.

Profile:
Cassia powder is distinctly sweeter and more robust than cinnamon. Its primary taste notes are **cinnamon-sugar** and **wet cedar** with a tail of **honeyed chilli**. Its strength, spice, and sweetness makes it an obvious winner in baking. Just watch out for its recessed **bitterness**: follow quantity advice carefully.

Form:
A densely powdered spice with a texture more akin to turmeric powder than cinnamon powder. It has a distinct warm ochre colour.

IN COOKING:
Cassia powder is commonly mislabelled and sold as cinnamon: technically known as "cassia cinnamon", it's a less costly spice than true cinnamon and the retail market profits from both the loophole and the general buyer's lack of education around spice. For this reason, many of us are familiar with its taste but not its correct name. Having said that, cassia powder is an entirely different spice from cinnamon powder. As an aromatic cassia powder is opulent: its very sugared, round, and pungent heat brings instant density and a deep warmth. Cassia powder makes the heat of chilli humid. It sweetens the blunt pungency of clove and nutmeg. Cassia powder chimes beautifully with tomato and pumpkin-based dishes such as tagines. A little bit of cassia powder in an eggplant moussaka creates a richer finish. It is a natural match with custard-style desserts that derive their foundation from egg yolk flavours. In baked goods, cassia powder works well with heavier, nutty flours, or in rustic fruit pies.

QUANTITY:
One-third to one-half teaspoon in dishes feeding four to six people.

USE WITH:
Cinnamon powder. Fine pink salt. Bay leaf. Fenugreek powder. Red chilli powder.

Replace with:
Equal parts cinnamon powder and clove powder.

Also called:
Jangli dalchini. Chinese cinnamon. Poor man's cinnamon.

Cayenne Pepper

CATEGORY:
Hot spice.

PROFILE:
Cayenne pepper puts forward a **dry** and **flat desert heat** that has a **dusty ash** character. Its secondary aromas are vaguely **bay leaf** and **dried herbaceous** in character. Absent is the floral quality present in many other varieties of chilli.

FORM:
A dark brick-coloured powder with a coarse grind.

IN COOKING:
Everyone has cayenne pepper stashed in the pantry, so let's get using. The dry, flat heat of cayenne pepper makes it ideal for dishes that require a strong contrast to pretty aromas or dishes that favour darker, drier aromatic

overtones. Cayenne pepper is a perfect match for the many regional Mexican dishes that are characterised by earthy tones: think of the classic molé. While it provides "lift" like other *hot* category spices, cayenne pepper is not a "bright" aromatic addition. Use cayenne pepper in pork and bean mixes where the spice works as a darker contrast to pork's sweet flavour. Cayenne pepper also matches the flat intensity of beef: it is a wonderful "barbecue" spice to include in marinades or dry meat rubs.

QUANTITY:
One-third to one-half teaspoon in dishes feeding four to six people.

USE WITH:
Cumin powder. Cumin seed. Oregano. Black pepper. Tomato. White salt. Honey. Soy.

REPLACE WITH:
Equal parts smoked paprika and red chilli powder.

Chilli Powder Kashmiri

CATEGORY:
Hot spice.

PROFILE:
Kashmiri chilli is native to Kashmir and used in Kashmiri Pandit cuisine in the powdered form to add colour and a mild heat. Kashmiri chilli powder has a heat that is **humid** and **floral** with strong brush of **smoke**. It is a classic, pretty chilli with recessed **salt** and a soft but very **"red" heat**.

FORM:
Orange-red dense powder with a heavy texture similar to cassia and turmeric powders.

IN COOKING:
Kashmiri chilli powder is such a joy to use. Its soft heat makes it ideal for people who struggle with hotter chillies, or for caregivers acclimatising a child's palate to heat. But it has a bigger role to play than just a "soft" chilli option. In traditional Kashmiri Pandit cooking Kashmiri chilli powder is used to add colour, and to provide aromatic length without overheating the classical dense, warm, earthy masala for which the region is known. It draws the sweetness forward in tomato, eggplant, and "orange" vegetables. Kashmiri chilli powder lightens a sugo, minimises pork's "feral" quality, and highlights the rich natural umami of lamb. Use it with black pepper, salt, cumin seed, and sumac to season roast vegetables and meat. A touch of Kashmiri chilli powder will reduce the bitterness in leafy greens. A pinch with fleur de sel creates an elegant milk chocolate mousse.

QUANTITY:
One-third to one teaspoon in dishes feeding four to six people.

USE WITH:
Cumin seed. Fine pink salt. Milk chocolate. Yellow mustard seed. Red chilli powder. Fine white pepper. Amchur. Cinnamon powder.

Replace with:
Equal parts smoked paprika and sweet paprika, alongside a quarter part of ground red chilli.

Also called:
Kashmiri mirch.

Chilli Powder Red

Category:
Hot spice.

Profile:
A classic red chilli powder can grade in heat from very mild to bushfire-burn. Classic Indian-style red chilli powder is characterised by a very **floral** quality pushed forward by **brick smoke**. Its heat is complex: ranging from **humid** at first taste to **dry tropic sun** as the hum of fire fades.

Form:
Varied shades of red and textural powder depending on the type of chilli.

In cooking:
Red chilli powder is useful for more than just making food "spicy". Like hot air rising, chilli lifts other aromas

up high. This is easiest to taste when red chilli powder is paired with creamy fats like coconut oil or coconut cream: it will "brighten" the dish by lifting the weight of fat off the bottom of the palate. A red chilli powder will lend an appearance of acidity to sticky, rich, and slow-cooked proteins. It pretties up pork with a floral punch. Lightens the metallic twang of beef. Including red chilli powder in a masala means you can get more complicated and textural with your spices: if you want to experiment with nutmeg powder, fennel seed, cumin powder, clove, and a little fenugreek powder, the ubiquitous sweet heat of a classic red chilli powder will lend unfamiliar flavour combinations a more familiar appearance.

QUANTITY:
One-third to one teaspoon in dishes feeding four to six people.

USE WITH:
Mace powder. Garlic. Fresh ginger. Fennel seed. Indian black salt. Clove buds. Sumac.

REPLACE WITH:
Equal parts fresh red chilli, Kashmiri chilli powder, and cayenne pepper.

ALSO CALLED:
Mirch.

Cinnamon Powder

CATEGORY:
Warm spice.

PROFILE:
True cinnamon in its whole form presents as a whorled and fine quill. Once ground there is a **tight** and **woody** aromatic quality to cinnamon powder that comes before the **sweetness** and **warmth** associated with this spice. Cinnamon powder is aromatically **restrained**, however its character is released through tempering.

FORM:
A fine powder that is the colour of warm clay.

IN COOKING:
I love cinnamon powder for its chameleon quality: depending on the companion spice, cinnamon can present

either as woody and "masculine" or warm and "feminine". Mediterranean spices and herbs such as oregano, parsley, and garlic bring forward cinnamon's darker, savoury qualities. *Hot* and *acidic* category spices shine a spotlight on cinnamon's "baked goods" sweetness. Use cinnamon powder in creamy sauces as a less astringent addition than nutmeg. Cinnamon powder highlights the savoury umami quality of lamb fat in a rogan josh or sticky lamb rib slow cook. Cinnamon powder is also interesting with soy sauce, garlic, fresh chilli, and molasses as a paste or marinade. In Kashmiri Pandit cooking cinnamon powder is used for warmth and density in sabzi and meat dishes. It forms part of a garam masala mix and is commonly used alongside ginger, turmeric, salt, cumin, and chilli as a foundational spice. Contrary to Western culinary tradition, regional Indian cooking doesn't consider cinnamon powder as a dessert spice. We use it as a savoury aromatic.

QUANTITY:
One-quarter to one-half teaspoon in dishes feeding four to six people.

USE WITH:
Star anise. Black pepper. Oregano. Clove buds. Tamarind. Jaggery. Fresh turmeric. Cassia powder.

REPLACE WITH:
Equal parts cassia powder and coriander powder.

ALSO CALLED:
Dalchini. True cinnamon. Sri Lankan cinnamon.

Cinnamon Quill

CATEGORY:
Structural spice.

PROFILE:
Like all structural category spices this is a difficult aromatic to taste raw. Cinnamon quill has a subtle **woody**, **baked goods** aroma. On the tongue, raw cinnamon quill tastes faintly of **clove cigarettes**. Possibly the most striking part of the cinnamon quill's profile is its **extreme subtlety**.

FORM:
A fine, tightly whorled, papery quill that is very pale tan in colour.

IN COOKING:
Like the other whole spices that form the *structural* spice category, cinnamon quills demand time in the pan in

order for the flavour to permeate a dish. The benefit of using the whole spice instead of the powder is the frame that cinnamon quills give: the tight and upright nature of the quill works like a "post" in the pan creating a central stability that allows other spices to be more fully expressed. The quills produce a complex aroma that harks of cedar as much as it does of baked cinnamon pastries. Unlike some other spices in this category, cinnamon quills are quite restrained which means they can be used in almost any dish where a touch of supported aromatic elegance is required.

Quantity:
One five-centimetre quill in dishes feeding four to six people.

Use with:
Cassia bark. Fresh turmeric. Fresh ginger. Cinnamon powder. Garam masala. Bay leaf. Green cardamom. Black cardamom.

Replace with:
Equal quantity of cassia bark and mace flower.

Also called:
Dalchini. True cinnamon. Sri Lankan cinnamon.

Coriander Leaf

CATEGORY:
Forest floor spice.

PROFILE:
Coriander leaf can elicit a strong reaction for some. But for those who enjoy it, coriander leaf is **fresh** with a soft **lemon rind** aroma and a faint kiss of **fine white pepper**.

FORM:
A ruffled, frog-green leaf with the appearance of a fairy's petticoat.

IN COOKING:
Try fresh coriander if you're looking for lemon-y without the lemon. As a general rule fresh coriander is much easier to integrate into contemporary dishes because it's

considered a finishing spice: like all fresh leaf spice, it is added at the end of the cooking process which means its aromatic contribution is very "top note". Top note spices are simpler to work with because they are typically gentler. Coriander leaf provides a freshness and a subtle lemon accent. It has a natural affinity with Mexican food and South Indian-style cuisine. Coriander leaf is great with subtly flavoured fish: it provides a citrus element that isn't overwhelming, chiefly because coriander leaf is not acidic. The fresh leaf harmonises with Mediterranean flavours. Any recipe that utilises tomato, olives, and capers will find a friend in fresh coriander. As a rule, if fresh coriander leaf isn't available then omit or try for fresh curry leaf: dried coriander is a less dimensional, harder, and more bitter expression of what is—in its fresh form—a beautiful and subtle herb.

Quantity:
Leaf spices have a lot of leeway when it comes to personal discretion: use fresh coriander "to taste" when adding it to food. As a rough guide, a small bunch added at the end of cooking will impact a dish feeding four to six people.

Use with:
Garlic. Onion. Mustard seeds. Red chilli powder. Fresh chillies. Tamarind. Coconut.

REPLACE WITH:
A combination of fresh curry leaf and coriander powder.

ALSO CALLED:
Taaja dhaniya. Cilantro.

Coriander Powder

Category:
Earth spice.

Profile:
Ground from the dried coriander seed, coriander powder does not elicit the same strength of reaction as coriander leaf. This is a **lightly herbaceous** spice with **soft lemon** and **chamomile** qualities. It has secondary notes of **soft loam** and **light dust**.

Form:
A fluffy ground powder of pollen-like texture that ranges in colour from soft and silvery beige to dark sand.

In cooking:
If you don't love coriander leaf, don't be scared to use coriander powder: this spice from the dried seed has none of the "soapy" qualities that some experience with the fresh

leaf. Just the opposite. Coriander powder is unusual for a dried spice in that it doesn't possess recessed qualities of pungency and bitterness. This is a very pretty aromatic that adds beautiful volume to a masala base, courtesy of the powder's fluffy and full texture. Because of its profile and the tendency to cook out quicker than other spices around it, coriander powder can be used in much greater volume than other dried powders. Aromatically somewhere between an *earth* spice and a *forest floor* spice, coriander powder combines those same functions in a pan: providing weight and texture for the mid-palate like an *earth* spice, while also moving flavour around the mouth like a *forest floor* spice. Use coriander powder in dishes that require the presence of earthiness without the cranky character of cumin powder. Coriander powder's volume also softens the flame of *hot* category spices making it a great inclusion in child-friendly spiced dishes. Try it in a chilli con carne to soften blunt edges. Or cook it with salt and a little turmeric in pan-fried potatoes to give kids a gentler starter experience with spice.

QUANTITY:
Two teaspoons in dishes feeding four to six people.

USE WITH:
Cumin seed. Fine pink salt. Coriander leaf. Turmeric powder. Cinnamon powder. Kashmiri chilli powder.

Replace with:
Equal parts ground cumin and amchur.

Also called:
Dhaniya.

Clove Buds

CATEGORY:
Structural spice.

PROFILE:
Clove birds have a distinct and strong aromatic character that combines **medicinal aniseed** with **hardwood** and **camphor**. The character is pungent with eager secondary profiles of **bitterness** and **heat**.

FORM:
A small club-shaped spice that is deep maroon-brown in colour and has a woody texture.

IN COOKING:
Clove buds penetrate a dish. Just like the club form they take, this is a strong spice and that's why Kashmiri Pandit cooks love it: unlike more delicate spice, clove buds handle high heat cooking without burning which means

they are often used in traditional Kashmiri meat dishes browned on high heat to build base structure. Western tradition literally sees them stud the Christmas ham. Being bold with clove buds isn't difficult, I actually think subtlety can be harder to navigate. Steer clear of olive oil and temper clove bud with a soft fat like ghee to mute its aroma. Use two to three clove buds in a chicken stuffing, or in slow cooked chicken dishes that retain chicken skin and bone: these richer aspects of poultry will offset some of clove's intensity. I love to use one or two clove buds in dairy-based dishes like paneer, béchamel sauce, or any white-sauced stew to add an edge of pungent warmth: it's quite easy for a white sauce to feel bland and fall flat. Try clove bud when cooking porridge. Clove buds are also surprisingly beautiful when paired with oily fish. Mackerel, clove buds, butter, fresh parsley, and salt and cracked black pepper is a fresh, peppery, and aniseedy mouthful.

QUANTITY:
One to three clove buds in dishes feeding four to six people if you're just starting out with clove buds. Three to six clove buds if you're more confident.

USE WITH:
Star anise. Kashmiri chilli powder. Fennel powder. Bay leaf. Pink salt. Indian black salt. Jaggery. Turmeric powder.

Replace with:
A combination of star anise (whole) and clove powder.

Also called:
Laung.

Clove Powder

CATEGORY:
Warm spice.

PROFILE:
Clove powder has a striking taste resemblance to its whole form, the clove bud: this is unusual in that most spices are diminished in aromatic intensity once ground. But not clove. Primary notes of **hot smoke** and **camphor**. Secondary characters segue to subtle **sweet apple pie** and a **blunt pepper aroma**.

FORM:
A dense powder that is bark brown in colour, with a heavy texture that is close to powdered clay.

IN COOKING:
Clove powder deserves more attention than as an ingredient in mixed spice, or in baking. It has a deep warmth that fills the mouth with more intensity than cassia or

cinnamon powders. Kashmiri Pandit cooking looks to clove powder for the depth it brings to savoury dishes. A winter dish of slow cooked beef cheeks will take on a more luscious character with the addition of a half teaspoon of clove powder: the spice will flesh out the stringy "metallic" quality of beef protein. Clove powder in a seafood chowder will harmonise the marriage between strong seafood and the sweetness of a dairy-based stock or sauce. I use clove powder with dried fenugreek leaf in methi chicken to bring dimension and warmth: chicken is a "light" protein and the movement of fenugreek leaf can leave a curry feeling too "thin" without the addition of a dense spice like clove powder. Its pungent character demands careful use: bitterness is just a pinch away.

QUANTITY:
One-quarter to a two-thirds teaspoon in dishes feeding four to six people.

USE WITH:
Curry leaf. Indian black salt. Pomegranate molasses. Ground red chilli. Fine white sea salt. Cassia bark. Nigella seed. Cumin seed.

REPLACE WITH:
A combination of nutmeg powder and clove buds.

ALSO CALLED:
Laung powder.

Cumin Powder

CATEGORY:
Earth spice.

PROFILE:
Cumin powder is the ground form of cumin seed but has a vastly different profile. While cumin seed is quite pretty and complex, cumin powder has a **flat** and **dusty** profile that tastes **soil-like** and **cranky**. It has a heavy texture, and its secondary and tertiary notes are sensations rather than tastes. Cumin powder **muffles** and **tamps down** higher-toned flavours in the way dirt does to a fire.

FORM:
A dull khaki powder with the fine texture of sandy soil.

IN COOKING:
If a recipe asks for cumin seed, cumin powder is not a replacement. These are two different spices. Cumin powder is a "dark" aromatic that contributes a pungent and

distinct earthy character. Too much will make a masala irreparably bitter. Use cumin powder in pumpkin soup to transform the one-dimensional sweetness of pumpkin into a flavour with more savoury interest. Cumin powder will bring depth to slow-cooked or roasted tomatoes. Similarly a pinch of cumin powder in a creamy omelette or buttery pan of scrambled eggs will reduce the feeling of richness. Cumin powder is well suited to chicken as a dry-rub with salt and pepper, and chilli, and it is a familiar component in Mexico where the traditional cuisine favours a very earthy spice expression. Use cumin powder in conjunction with cumin seed for an elegant cumin expression.

Quantity:
One-quarter to a two-thirds teaspoon in dishes feeding four to six people.

Use with:
Black mustard seed. Yellow mustard seed. Garlic. Curry leaf. Fresh turmeric. Fresh red chilli. Tamarind.

Replace with:
Equal parts coriander powder and caraway powder.

Also called:
Jeera powder.

Cumin Seed

CATEGORY:
Earth spice.

PROFILE:
Cumin seed is the whole form of this spice. It has **warm** and **woody** primary aromas that segue to **mint**, **eucalyptus**, and a residual **pungent cedar** quality. Cumin seed has a soft **bitter** finish. It is a complex spice given structure by its firm dried seed husk.

FORM:
An elongated seed with a fine tail and close, textured ribbing. Its colour is silvered khaki.

IN COOKING:
Who doesn't love cumin seed? Of all the spices in my classes it is the one most widely recognised and appreciated. Cumin seed is ubiquitous in Subcontinental,

Middle Eastern, and Mediterranean cultures. Its dual warm and cool aromatic nature—at once cedar and mint—means that cumin seed is a chameleon which blends with and enhances almost any spice mix. Cumin seed contributes textural interest and a "fullness" that the palate finds pleasing. Children largely find cumin seed palatable, making it a great aromatic when introducing them to more complex flavours: try starting off your spice junior with a classic yellow dal softly spiced with salt, turmeric, and cumin seed. Use cumin seed in everything from chicken soup, to rich tomato-based slow cooks in winter, to a classic gobi sabzi, and as a seasoning with salt and turmeric on fried eggs for breakfast.

QUANTITY:
One-half to two teaspoons in dishes feeding four to six people.

USE WITH:
Turmeric powder. Hot ground chilli. Ginger powder. Amchur. Cinnamon quills. Green cardamom. Coriander powder.

REPLACE WITH:
Equal parts cumin powder and aniseed.

ALSO CALLED:
Jeera.

Curry Leaf

Category:
Forest floor spice.

Profile:
Curry leaf is the leaf from the curry plant and is beautiful when picked and used fresh. The leaf has upfront primary character of **pepper** and **basil** that mellows to **almond** and subtle **sesame seed.** Secondary aromas include **cumquat rind** and **white pepper**.

Form:
Teardrop-shaped leaves evenly spaced on thin green stems. The leaves are a verdant young green.

In cooking:
Curry leaf tastes like India. It is a fragrant, fresh, and distinct addition to savoury dishes. My second son says it smells "sweet" and "green"—he struggles to enjoy the aroma. I love it. Like all fresh leaf spices, it is best added

at the end of the cooking process in order to preserve its delicate aromas. Curry leaf contributes a sweetness to foods as it has a unique sesame seed/almond flavour framed by a herbaceous basil quality. It pairs very well with tomato and classic Mediterranean flavours, as well as having an obvious symbiosis with South Indian cuisine. Curry leaf adds an exotic and compelling element to mussels cooked in tomato and white wine, and it is lovely in a simple dish of fish poached in coconut cream, salt, chilli, and fresh turmeric. If you can't find fresh curry leaf, in my mind it is better to go without: dried curry leaf has none of the fresh vibrancy, is aromatically "blunt", and can quite quickly become bitter. If you must use the dried version, reduce the quantity to just six to eight individual leaves in any one dish.

QUANTITY:
Two to three, three-inch long stems of fresh leaves in dishes feeding four to six people.

USE WITH:
Fresh turmeric. Fresh ginger. Fresh red chilli. Tamarind. Onion. Fine pink salt. Mustard seeds.

REPLACE WITH:
A combination of sesame seed and coriander leaf.

ALSO CALLED:
Karee patta.

Fennel Powder

Category:
Warm spice.

Profile:
A warm **Dutch liquorice** primary taste with a back note of **dusty cumin.** This is a much flatter version of fennel than the vibrant and textural fennel seed. A tertiary characteristic of **minced onion** gives fennel powder a touch of **recessed sulphur**.

Form:
A dense powder that is soft olive/khaki in colour and has a texture similar to nutmeg and clove powders.

In cooking:
I reach for fennel powder when I want to recreate "comfort" in a plate of food. Without the husk intact, the earthy liquorice sweetness associated with fennel seeds

devolves into a warmer and gentler spice that tucks a soft aniseed quality into the depths of a dish. Its impact is discrete: the full mouth feel created by fennel powder is more forward than its aromatic contribution. A "full mouth" signals satisfaction, while its soft quality removes any feeling of aromatic challenge. Satisfaction without challenge. Together these two sensations approximate the state of emotional safety. This sensory expression is what makes fennel powder a natural addition to classically comforting foods across all cultures. Kashmiri Pandit cooking utilises fennel powder in mutton rogan josh, thool zamboor (a rich egg curry), and kokur (chicken) rogan josh. Fennel powder is suited to cassoulets, moussakas, lasagnes, and baba ganouj. It is a gentle aromatic that can be added to mashed sweet potato or the British classic mushy peas when introducing young palates to spices. Another child-friendly spice to add to the list.

QUANTITY:
One-half to two teaspoons in dishes feeding four to six people.

USE WITH:
Garam masala. Clove buds. Ginger powder. Fine pink salt. Kashmiri chilli powder. Black cardamom. Yoghurt.

Replace with:
Aniseed powder.

Also called:
Saunf powder.

Fennel Seed

CATEGORY:
Earth spice.

PROFILE:
The whole form of this spice. Fennel seed is aromatically strong, therefore can be a divisive flavour. The seed has a primary character of **sweet** and **wet liquorice** that is followed by **salt** and a cool, **white mint** finish.

FORM:
A plump, elongated dried seed, soft-green in colour, with distinct ribbing and a fine tail.

IN COOKING:
I love fennel seed, it's such a giving spice. In its seed form, fennel has a complex, sweet anise flavour and an unctuous chew. Unlike many other dried aromatic seeds, fennel retains a soft and slightly sticky texture very different to the pungent, desiccated mouthfeel of cumin

seeds. And yet despite the sweet profile, fennel seed has a strong push in even the most complex masala. There are three ways to use fennel seed to best effect. The first instance is to spotlight fennel seed's sweet liquorice profile in simple dishes with strong flavour: a classic pork and fennel sausage, for example, as a dry rub with salt and pepper on pork crackling, or alongside sugar and salt in an Italian almond flour and fennel seed sweet biscuit. To moderate fennel seed's impact but make the most of its sweetness in savoury dishes, pair it with fennel powder, aniseed, or aniseed powder: the density of the ground spices will soften fennel seed's texture and so "shorten" its aroma. It won't persist in the mouth as long. Try this combination of spice alongside salt and pepper, bay leaf, turmeric powder, chilli powder, and fresh garlic in a lamb casserole or slow cook. To minimise fennel seed's liquorice sweetness and draw forward its latent salt and white mint qualities, pair with green cardamom, salt, fine white pepper, and fenugreek powder in pea and ham soup for a lighter, more savoury iteration of this winter soup classic.

QUANTITY:
One-half to one teaspoon in dishes feeding four to six people.

USE WITH:
Pink salt. Cinnamon powder. Ginger powder. Ground cumin. Kashmiri red chilli. Fenugreek seed. Fresh turmeric.

Replace with:
Aniseed.

Also called:
Saunf.

Fenugreek Leaf (Dried)

CATEGORY:
Forest floor spice.

PROFILE:
Fenugreek leaf is from the fenugreek plant, a spinach-like bitter green with leaves that can be eaten dried or fresh. In the dried form, fenugreek leaves have an **overripe sweetness** with notes of **pepper** and **sandalwood**. This aromatic has a lingering and **broadly bitter** finish.

FORM:
Small, brittle, and square-ish leaves bunched in unruly clumps. The dried leaves are a dark, flat forest green.

IN COOKING:
Fenugreek leaf is a great starting point for fenugreek newbies: it is the friendliest of the fenugreek forms with the

softest aromatic impact, and is a great way to get familiar with a trio of spices (leaf/seed/powder) that are little known inside domestic Western cooking circles. The sweet, peppery quality of fenugreek leaf makes it a natural match with lamb, chicken, and fish. Outside of classic Indian regional cooking, consider adding fenugreek leaf to dishes where basil and oregano would find a natural home. Using fenugreek leaf to replace these herbs will add an exotic twist without disturbing the known taste profiles. Try it in chicken cacciatore; any seafood dish served with slow-cooked tomato; or lamb dishes that feature garlic, onion, and lemon. Like all *forest floor* category spices, fenugreek leaf adds "movement" to a masala, so it works well with dense aromatics like fennel and nutmeg powders. Fenugreek leaf moves flavour around the palate which makes complex and full masalas less confronting, as well as more digestible.

Quantity:
One to two tablespoons in dishes feeding four to six people.

Use with:
Black pepper. Turmeric powder. Fresh green chillies. Yoghurt. Jaggery. Fenugreek powder. Ginger powder. Fresh ginger. Fennel seed. Clove bud.

Replace with:
Tulsi (Holy basil).

Also called:
Kasoori methi.

Fenugreek Powder

CATEGORY:
Bitter spice.

PROFILE:
Fenugreek powder is the ground form of the fenugreek seed. Fenugreek seed comes from the fenugreek plant but has a much more stronger bitter presentation, hence its inclusion in the *bitter* spice category. Fenugreek powder has **bitter celery leaf** and **apple seed** primary notes that are followed by a **strychnine** aftertaste. Subtle secondary and tertiary notes of **liquorice** and **lemon rind** create a pleasing, palatable frame.

FORM:
A dense powder with a very smooth, dry-paste texture that is rich cream in colour.

IN COOKING:
Fenugreek powder is generally the spice bought for a one-off curry and then forgotten. Its use outside of traditional regional Indian recipe can feel obscure. Let's correct that. As a *bitter* category spice, fenugreek powder finds its best expression in the base flavour of a dish. One of its most powerful impacts is the ability of fenugreek powder to create a strong spine that "holds up" heavy flavours: our enjoyment of a meal is negatively impacted if a mouthful feels heavy. By including a strong aromatic spine, "heavy" becomes "rich" and that sensation of "too much" becomes "delicious". With this in mind, consider using fenugreek powder in tomato- and beef-based slow braises, satisfying vegetarian stews, cassoulet-style dishes, and even small amounts (less than a third of a teaspoon) in heavy desserts like cheesecake and milk chocolate mousse. This last addition will lighten the feel of a dessert without interfering with its richness. Fenugreek powder is also excellent in umami-rich dishes as a strong bitter counterpoint to all of that sweet richness.

QUANTITY:
One-quarter to one-half teaspoon in dishes feeding four to six people.

USE WITH:
Fenugreek leaf. White pepper. Black pepper. Kashmiri chilli. Turmeric powder. Pink salt. Indian black salt. Pomegranate molasses. Fennel seed. Cassia bark.

REPLACE WITH:
A combination of turmeric powder and fresh garlic.

ALSO CALLED:
Methi.

Fenugreek Seed

CATEGORY:
Bitter spice.

PROFILE:
Fenugreek seed is the seed form of the fenugreek plant. Its primary notes are buffered by the seed's pebble-like texture—this is a difficult spice to taste. Once penetrated with the teeth, fenugreek seed has a taste of **apple skin** that gives way to **almond shell** and a slightly sweet finish of **old apple flesh**. Secondary notes reference aromas of **yellow mustard seed.** A very recessed **maple syrup** quality comes forward when the seed is heated.

FORM:
A stout square seed that is as hard as a pebble and tan/yellow in colour.

IN COOKING:
Fenugreek seed is added to traditional Indian pickles and acidic relishes as a preservative and stabiliser. It makes a strong digestive "tea" when steeped in hot water with cumin and fennel seeds. Sprouting the seeds and using the sprouts to top salads is also a delicious and naturally medicinal way to consume this spice.

QUANTITY:
Varies depending on your pickle recipe. In a digestive tea for one person, use one-half teaspoon.

USE WITH:
Cumin seed and fennel seed in tea. Mustard seed, salt, black pepper, and chillies in pickles.

REPLACE WITH:
An equal blend of fenugreek powder and yellow mustard seed.

ALSO CALLED:
Methi.

Galangal Fresh

Category:
Astringent-sulphuric spice.

Profile:
Fresh galangal is a rhizome that is often confused for ginger but has a firmer texture, a darker "tiger" stripe on the skin, and is a much more astringent and domineering taste. Primary characters include strong frontal aromas of **tiger balm**, **lavender**, and **ginger** that fade to a secondary aroma of **ground mace.**

Form:
A rhizome with a pinkish-ginger colour that has a harder texture and rougher appearance than ginger.

In cooking:
Fresh galangal is a dynamic, hot, and driving "wet" spice that slices through dense aromatics and accelerates *hot*

and *acidic* spices like a rollercoaster running a triple loop. Its strident nature makes it a natural pairing with beef: as a protein, beef requires a lot of aromatic punch to shift its heavy metallic quality, and galangal has this ability. Because fresh galangal is so distinct, it is advisable to contain its use to South East Asian or Asian dishes. Try it in a massaman or jungle style curry. Fresh galangal is great for wok cooking because its slightly tough flesh makes it less inclined to burn or be damaged aromatically by very high heat.

QUANTITY:
A 10 to 20 gram piece in dishes feeding four to six people.

USE WITH:
Fresh turmeric. Green chilli. Black pepper. Coconut cream. Lemongrass. Red chilli powder. Turmeric powder. Tamarind.

REPLACE WITH:
A combination of fresh ginger and fresh turmeric.

ALSO CALLED:
Thai ginger. Blue ginger.

Galangal Powder

CATEGORY:
Warm spice.

PROFILE:
The ground incarnation of fresh galangal is a subtler proposition than whole, fresh galangal though it still retains a distinct aromatic profile and is a more complex dried spice than many. Primary aromas are **powdered sandalwood**, **pepper**, and **lavender**. These segue to **oil** and **ginger**. There are recessed **salt** and **rosemary** qualities.

FORM:
An oily powder with a smooth texture, the colour of clotted cream.

IN COOKING:
This is possibly the least used spice in my kitchen. The distinct character of galangal is one I use rarely: its profile clashes with traditional Kashmiri Pandit flavours. Lovers

of South East Asian or Chinese-Malay food will find much more use for this spice. Like its fresh incarnation, galangal powder packs an immense aromatic punch but in the dried form it is much warmer and rounder. Use it in small quantities in the base of a masala—alongside ginger and turmeric powders—to lift and emphasise the round floral quality of both of the companion spices. Galangal powder has a tenderising quality that works well with lemon juice, garlic, and yoghurt in marinades. In any sweet dish that calls for ginger powder, substitute one third of that measure with galangal powder to add a hint of lavender and a rich, viscose texture to sweet baked goods.

Quantity:
One-quarter to one-half teaspoon in dishes feeding four to six people.

Use with:
White pepper. Red chilli powder. Lime. Fresh ginger. Fresh green chilli. Clove powder. Pink salt. Indian black salt. Turmeric powder.

Replace with:
A balanced combination of ginger powder, mace powder, and turmeric powder.

Also called:
Thai ginger. Blue ginger.

Garam Masala

Category:
Warm spice.

Profile:
Garam masala in the powdered form is a blend of whole spices ground together to form this warm and pungent spice blend. Garam masala literally means "warm spice". It typically includes bay leaf, nutmeg, clove, cumin seed, fennel seed, and cinnamon though each region—each family—in India has its own special recipe. Some garam masala blends can include upward of 12 spices. Generally speaking, primary characters of **soil** and **floral** aromas give way to a **biscuity warmth** and a finish of **dried sweet raisin**.

Form:
A clove-brown powder that has a dense weight and fluffy texture.

IN COOKING:
Garam masala is flexible as a spice. It can be used in so many different ways and each method has a different aromatic impact. Used in the base of a masala, it contributes a very dense and textured warmth: aromatically, this translates as a rich and pungent spice flavour. Think of using it in winter ragus or chicken casserole slow cooks to strengthen the underbelly of the dish. When used as a finishing spice, garam masala is much prettier. For example, the traditional practice of adding garam masala to a simple yellow dal at the end of cooking "refreshes" the more heavily cooked spice in the depths of the dish. Spicing with garam masala in this style is a great match to fish and shellfish dishes that require a lighter touch. Because of garam masala's inherent warmth it takes quite a significant mistake in terms of overuse for this spice to default to bitterness. Still, it's wise to be a little sparing particularly when adding as a finishing touch as its biscuity raisin sweetness can overwhelm subtler aromas.

QUANTITY:
One-half to one teaspoon in dishes feeding four to six people.

USE WITH:
Ginger powder. Clove buds. Cinnamon quill. Kashmiri chilli powder. Turmeric powder. Fennel powder. Bay leaf. Pink salt. Black cardamom.

REPLACE WITH:
Equal parts mace powder, cumin powder, and clove powder.

Garlic Fresh

Category:
Astringent-sulphuric spice.

Profile:
The taste profile of fresh garlic is so well known to most that its aromatic description would appear redundant. But breaking down its components allows further understanding of how and when to pair this fresh spice. Primary characters of **macadamia** and **hazelnut** flash through **butter** before being swamped by **green onion stalk**. The **soft minerality** of **spring water** is a secondary characteristic.

Form:
A small bulb with crescent-shaped cloves varying in colour from textured cream through to pink and soft purple.

IN COOKING:
The beauty of garlic is more than its sweetly sulphuric, green, and acidic flavour contribution. Garlic freshens and brightens dark and complex spice combinations, allowing pungent masalas to sit a little easier on the palate. Like onion, fresh ginger, and fresh galangal, garlic lends food a bright "summer" energy that is stimulating and enlivening. Classic Kashmiri Pandit cooking doesn't use garlic, but its presence in tamarind- and coconut-based dishes from the Southern Indian regions is lovely.

QUANTITY:
Two to six cloves in dishes feeding four to six people.

USE WITH:
Onion. Curry leaf. Fresh turmeric. Fresh ginger. Cumin seed. Fresh red or green chilli. Garam masala. Nigella seed. Jaggery. Coriander powder.

REPLACE WITH:
Asafoetida.

Ginger Fresh

CATEGORY:
Astringent-sulphuric spice.

PROFILE:
Fresh ginger is ubiquitous in Subcontinental and South East Asian cooking and is prized for its **sweet**, **wet**, and **astringent** contribution to savoury spiced foods. It has primary aromatic qualities of **candlenut** and **freesia** followed by **kaffir lime** and a finish of **garlicky acidity.**

FORM:
A knobbly rhizome varying in colour from pale cream to dirty iced coffee: the fresher the rhizome, the thinner its skin and paler its colour.

IN COOKING:
Fresh ginger is wet and astringent, yet it retains a warmth and weight that marries beautifully with Asian spicing. Whereas the sulphuric qualities of garlic and onion

somewhat "deconstruct" dense aromatic architecture, fresh ginger brings a bright relief to a dish without interfering with the texture and density of the spice. Fresh ginger's sweet, citric, earthy, and subtle mineral qualities create harmonious interactions with all aromatics, making it an easy spice to adapt to both sweet and savoury dishes. I love fresh ginger in sweet ricotta fritters made with a fresh ginger syrup. Fresh ginger brightens a traditional Kashmiri gajar matar sabzi (spiced carrot with peas), and long slivers of ginger that have enough surface area to withstand high heat can be the start of any easy mid-week stir fried wok dish.

QUANTITY:
One to three teaspoons of minced ginger in dishes feeding four to six people.

USE WITH:
Turmeric powder. Fresh turmeric. Cassia powder. Cumin powder. Coriander powder. Sumac. Cumin seed. Kashmiri chilli powder. Pink salt. White pepper. Coriander leaf.

REPLACE WITH:
A combination of fresh galangal and ginger powder.

ALSO CALLED:
Adarak.

Ginger Powder

Category:
Warm spice.

Profile:
This is another case of change the spice form, change the spice category: ginger powder is a subtler and rounder spice than fresh ginger. **Wood** and **sand** are the strong primary notes followed by **rose** and **oil**. There is a secondary **orange rind** quality and a fragrant tail of **fine white pepper**.

Form:
A substantial powder. Like turmeric, it has a slightly oily quality when touched and the powder often has two tiers of texture: a sandy-weight of powder threaded with dried fibrous filaments. Its colour is pale and golden tan.

In cooking:
Ginger powder has a powerfully warm presence that sits deep in a dish. It draws spice forward to the front

palate and "rounds out" a dish's aromatic structure. It can draw forth latent sweet and floral qualities in chillies, enhance the warmth of cinnamon, or help structure savoury masala dishes. In Western cuisine, it's frequently confined to sweet puddings and cakes. But it's more versatile than that. Try it with black pepper and fresh parsley in a savoury tart or quiche. With a little jaggery, salt, butter, chilli, and turmeric powder, ginger powder is a lovely spice mix for delicate shellfish.

QUANTITY:
One-third to one teaspoon in dishes feeding four to six people.

USE WITH:
Fennel powder. Aniseed. Green cardamom pods. Kashmiri chilli powder. Fenugreek powder. Amchur. Fresh fenugreek leaf.

REPLACE WITH:
A combination of equal parts turmeric powder and galangal powder.

ALSO CALLED:
Adarak.

Jaggery

CATEGORY:
Sweet spice.

PROFILE:
Made from cane sugar syrup, jaggery is a rich and complex sugar that is prized for its texture and soft sweetness. Primary characters are **caramel**, **butterscotch**, and **butter**. **Molasses** and **honey** secondary characters add texture and complexity.

FORM:
Commonly sold either as a block or in rounds, this type of jaggery varies in colour from honeyed-caramel to a darker rapadura-brown. Generally, the more honeyed the colour the sweeter and more caramelised the flavour. As the sugar block darkens, expect deeper notes of bitter molasses to step forward.

IN COOKING:
Jaggery is a sugar that eats like a dessert, just on its own. Because it is minimally refined, jaggery has a fuller, richer sweetness than other sugars. Its buttery quality makes jaggery ideal for use in complex spice blends when the tension created by aromatic contrasts calls for a counterbalance. The best example of jaggery is to use a small amount to soften the pungent quality of ajwain or the sharp heat found in the combination of garlic, onion, and red chilli. When using jaggery in its block form, add the cut pieces to the base of the masala: the heat and the fat will soften the jaggery enough that it will break apart at the press of a wooden spoon and can be evenly stirred through. Jaggery powder is simpler to use, but that one extra step of refining the sugar reduces some of its dimension. Jaggery is also a great addition to masala when cooking for children. The old adage of "a spoon of sugar" as it relates to medicine, holds up with spice: using a little bit of jaggery in a simple spice blend for kids will help a young palate to acclimatise to complex flavour. Reduce the quantity of jaggery gradually as the child becomes more comfortable with aromatic contrast. Across India, jaggery is also combined with ghee to make rich traditional desserts, like a peanut brittle style treat called chikki or gajak made with peanuts or sesame seeds.

Quantity:
1.5 cm x 1.5 cm piece in dishes feeding four to six people.

Use with:
Fennel seed. Fresh turmeric. Fresh ginger. Cumin seed. Red chilli powder. Coriander leaf. Coriander powder. Mace powder. Tamarind.

Replace with:
Palm sugar. Coconut sugar. Rapadura.

Also called:
Gur.

Lemon Fresh

CATEGORY:
Acidic spice.

PROFILE:
Everyone knows lemon juice. Its primary aromatic notes are **fresh water**, **lemonade** and **sunshine**. It has a secondary quality of **salt**.

FORM:
A baseball sized, teardrop-shaped citrus fruit, ranging in colour from pale to sunshine yellow.

IN COOKING:
Like all "wet" acids, fresh lemon has a powerful ability to "split" spice. Used with the Lebanese seven bharat spice—similar in taste to a garam masala—lemon juice pulls apart the pungent qualities of nutmeg, allspice, and clove, allowing the subtler spicing of coriander seed to

shine through. Lemon juice is great as a protein tenderiser in marinades, particularly when using meat cuts that contain minimal fat. Lemon rind offers a bitter edge to dishes rich with umami: the finishing gremolata mix of parsley and lemon rind on an osso bucco is a great example of this.

QUANTITY:
One-quarter to one-half of a lemon will make a big impact in dishes feeding four to six people.

USE WITH:
Garlic. Onion. Curry leaf. Mustard oil. Jaggery. Hot ground red chilli. Ajwain. Cumin powder. Jaggery.

REPLACE WITH:
A combination of lime and a gentle vinegar.

Lime Fresh

CATEGORY:
Acidic spice.

PROFILE:
Lime is a much prettier offering than its cousin the lemon. Primary **salt** and **acidic floral** characters are at the forefront. There are recessed qualities of **sweet liquorice** and **oyster shell**.

FORM:
A golf ball-sized citrus, varying in colour from lime-yellow to forest green.

IN COOKING:
The sweeter quality of lime translates into a softer effect on spice than its close cousin, the lemon. When using fresh lime in a masala, introduce it at the midway point of the cooking process: after creating a marriage between

the produce, fats, and spices in the base of the dish, add a squeeze of lime juice to establish a sweet and fresh acidic brightness in the middle. Continue to cook the dish, adding tomato puree, coconut cream, or yoghurt for density, and a pinch of a warm and dense spice like garam masala on top to seal it. This method shows the prettiness of the lime to its best advantage.

Quantity:
One-quarter to one-half of a lime will make a big impact in dishes feeding four to six people.

Use with:
Fresh red chilli. Coconut cream. Tamarind. Fresh galangal. Garlic. Lemongrass. Fresh green chilli. White salt.

Replace with:
Lemon.

Mace Flower

Category:
Structural spice.

Profile:
The mace flower is the outer covering of the nutmeg kernel. It is a visually beautiful aromatic: bright tangerine-red when fresh with a very pretty shape. But like nutmeg, it has very strong aromatic properties. Primary characters are dominant and taste of **menthol**, **orange rind** and **saddle leather**.

Form:
A pretty peach-coloured dried "flower" that resembles a miniature water lily. It is frilled and filigreed.

In cooking:
Like all *structural* spices, mace flower is best used in the base of a masala to give it time to release. Contrary to

its name, mace flower is far more than simply "floral." It imparts a subtle orange rind aroma to dishes as well as a leathery textural quality. Most spices require partnering with other spices in order to establish a full mouthfeel, but mace flower achieves that job on its own. Experiment with mace flower by throwing a single dried blossom into the base of any dish to see what it contributes. Because mace flower straddles the aromatic profiles of nutmeg, orange, and clove, it finds a home across all cuisines. Use it in cream-based Western European dishes, with galangal in South East Asian dishes, with tomato and fresh oregano in Mediterranean cuisines, or with sumac in Middle Eastern dishes.

QUANTITY:
One flower in dishes feeding four to six people.

USE WITH:
Garam masala. Black cardamom. Turmeric powder. Ginger powder. Pink salt. Curry leaf. Ghee. Cinnamon powder. Kashmiri chilli powder.

REPLACE WITH:
Equal parts nutmeg powder and turmeric powder.

ALSO CALLED:
Javitri.

Mace Powder

CATEGORY:
Warm spice.

PROFILE:
Mace powder is the ground form of the mace flower. Mace flower forms the outer protection of the nutmeg kernel. Just like is the case with clove, the aromatic similarity between the whole and the powdered form of mace is strikingly similar: even as a ground spice mace retains much of its power. Primary characters are **saddle leather** and **orange rind**, chased by a secondary **stripe of mint**. Its tertiary character offers an anaesthetic quality that faintly **numbs** the tongue.

FORM:
A peachy-orange powder with a fluffy and heavy texture comparable to garam masala.

IN COOKING:
The orange rind quality of mace powder makes this a really useable spice. Traditionally mace powder is used in Kashmiri Pandit cooking for its dense, floral, and pungent qualities. It adds depth to the classic KP spice combination of ginger powder, Kashmiri chilli powder, whole cloves, and cassia powder. Although it's less well-known in Western cooking, the orange rind quality of mace powder makes this a really usable spice. But like its close cousin nutmeg it has a lot of aromatic strength so use it in small amounts. It is a match with white-fleshed proteins like veal, chicken, and seafood. It's delicious with crustaceans. Cooking over charcoal beautifully balances mace powder so try it with chargrilled crayfish or langoustines, paired with a little salt, fresh lime, chilli, and garlic. If you are steaming fish, use just a little as mace will dominate. Mace powder can also work in cream-based sauces: it is a lighter and brighter alternative to the darker tones of nutmeg.

QUANTITY:
One-third to one teaspoon in dishes feeding four to six people.

USE WITH:
Fennel seed. Cinnamon powder. Turmeric powder. Fresh red chilli. Fresh ginger. Coconut milk.

Replace with:
Equal parts of nutmeg powder and turmeric powder.

Also called:
Javitri.

Mustard Seed Black

Category:
Astringent-sulphuric spice.

Profile:
These small black seeds are known for their pop when they hit heat and oil in the frying pan. Tasted as a raw spice, they are quite restrained. Primary aromas of **raw pea** and **rancid hazelnut** open to secondary characters of **green pea shoot** and **light soil**. With black mustard seed the tertiary character is that sensation of **oral spaciousness** facilitated by *astringent-sulphuric* category spice. The application of heat and fat draws forward black mustard seed's **heating** quality.

Form:
Small, matte black seeds that are larger than poppy seeds but smaller than coriander seeds.

IN COOKING:
Black mustard seed is probably one of the most universally recognised flavours of India. It forms part of the masala known as panch phoran (an Indian five spice) and is used extensively across the South Indian regions alongside garlic, turmeric, and mustard oil. This spice is a natural inclusion in seafood dishes with curry leaf and coconut cream. In a non-traditional context, use it in pumpkin soup: when heated, the sweet, pungent, and nutty qualities of mustard seed are beautiful companions to this delicious autumnal vegetable.

QUANTITY:
One-half to two teaspoons in dishes feeding four to six people.

USE WITH:
Fresh green chilli. Yellow mustard seed. Garlic. Curry leaf. Fresh ginger. Fresh turmeric. Aniseed powder.

REPLACE WITH:
Equal parts yellow mustard seed and nigella seed.

ALSO CALLED:
Rai or sarson.

Mustard Seed Yellow

CATEGORY:
Astringent-sulphuric spice.

PROFILE:
Yellow mustard seed is a subtler profile than black mustard seed. Though it contributes a similar nutty quality to the pan, it has softer heat and mellower aromatic character: primary notes of **summer hay** and **toasted bread** evolve to secondary characters of **fresh almond**. The finish of yellow mustard seed has a gentle, **young green onion** quality.

FORM:
Small seeds that are larger than poppy seeds but smaller than coriander seeds, ranging in colour from yellow to light tan.

IN COOKING:
Traditionally I would pair yellow and black mustard seed in classic South Indian seafood dishes for a more textured mustard seed impact. But because yellow mustard seed is less bitter and pungent than black mustard seed it can be easily used in non-traditional ways without overwhelming a non-Indian cuisine. Yellow mustard seed will add zing to a béchamel and works well with tomato-based dishes that feature fresh basil or oregano. It is a subtle aroma that adds impact to hazelnut and honey-roasted chicken, and could even be added in small quantities to toasted granola and homemade muesli bar mixes.

QUANTITY:
One-half to two teaspoons in dishes feeding four to six people.

USE WITH:
Fresh green chilli. Black mustard seed. Garlic. Curry leaf. Fresh ginger. Fresh turmeric. Aniseed powder.

REPLACE WITH:
Black mustard seed.

ALSO CALLED:
Rai or sarson.

Nigella Seed

CATEGORY:
Earth spice.

PROFILE:
Nigella seed is one of those spices that, like mustard seeds, releases its aroma through heat. As a raw spice it is a subtler tasting experience. Obvious primary aromas include **charcoal** and **soot** with a **sesame seed** finish. Secondary characters invoke a rancid **garlic high note**. As a tertiary experience, nigella seed offers the sensation of **oral emptiness** owing to the hidden sulphuric quality that comes to the fore when this spice is heated.

FORM:
A charcoal-black, teardrop-shaped seed that is matte in texture.

IN COOKING:
Nigella seed is a versatile team player of a spice and—when heated—has a subtle onion sweetness that draws forward nutty and sulphuric qualities from the spices around it. For this reason it is found in panch phoran (Indian five spice). In Kashmiri Pandit cooking it is combined with cumin and fennel seeds for making lamb and mutton curries. But it's versatility translates across many cuisines. Nigella seed is a natural addition to flatbread—lots of you will know it from its role as a Turkish bread garnish—and brings a toasted element to pumpkin and sweet potato when roasted on top of the vegetables with salt and oil. Try it in rich winter beef slow cooks, whisk it through omelettes with chilli and salt, or use a small proportion in a delicate shellfish dish prepared with butter and fine white pepper.

QUANTITY:
One-half to one teaspoon in dishes feeding four to six people.

USE WITH:
Cumin seed. Ground cumin. Fennel seed. Ginger powder. Asafoetida. Yoghurt. Clove buds. Star anise. Black cardamom. Coriander leaf.

Replace with:
A combination of fresh onion and fenugreek seed.

Also called:
Kalonji. Black cumin.

Nutmeg Powder

CATEGORY:
Warm and *astringent-sulphuric* spice.

PROFILE:
Nutmeg powder is the only spice in the Companion to get a two category coding. This is because its volume has it behave like a *warm* spice. Its overarching bitter and sharp character has it behave as an *astringent-sulphuric* spice. Tasting notes are equally contrasting. Primary character that is equal parts **clove**, **mint** and **bitter chocolate**. Secondary characters are **bitter onion** tailed by faint **apple-seed**. Its tertiary shape is both **warm** and **full**, and **sharp** and **clearing**.

FORM:
A very fine brown powder with a fluffy texture similar to mace powder and garam masala.

IN COOKING:
Nutmeg powder is so much more than a sprinkle on your banana smoothie. It is a powerful and pungent spice with multiple uses. In Indian cooking broadly, nutmeg powder brings shade and complexity to masala. In traditional Kashmiri Pandit spicing it is used in small amounts to produce tonal depth in cinnamon powder, whole clove, and mace powder. I use it when I want to make an intense gobi sabzi. But I also reach for it to balance "non-Indian" dishes. Paired with dairy it has an astringent impact and provides welcome contrast to cheesy sauces and milk-based desserts. Paired with sweet or rich produce like tomato or pumpkin it has a warm impact: it adds a rich feel to tagines and vegetable stews. Consider pairing nutmeg with fresh parsley, cream, black pepper, and fresh oregano to create a flavour base for oven bakes.

QUANTITY:
One-third to one-half teaspoon in dishes feeding four to six people.

USE WITH:
Mace flower. Turmeric powder. Fresh red chilli. Jaggery. Tamarind. Coconut milk. Ghee. Fennel seed. Amchur. Curry leaf.

Replace with:
Equal parts mace powder and clove powder.

Also called:
Jaiphal.

Onion Fresh

Category:
Astringent-sulphuric spice.

Profile:
For the sake of efficacy I'm writing up onions as a single entry, though different onions have different profiles. White onions are very **sharp** and **wet**. Brown onions appear **earthier**. Purple or red salad onions offer a softer **sulphur-sweet** profile that sits higher in the gullet.

Form:
A roundish bulb varying in colour from white through to brown, purple, and red, with layers to its heart like those of a Babushka doll.

In cooking:
It feels safe to say that even the most low-key cook knows how to work with onion, so I'll spend my words advising

both when its best to refrain from using onions with spices, and how to use onions in extravagant fashion. Kashmiri Pandit cooking traditionally doesn't use garlic or onion at all so steer clear of this aromatic when making classic KP dishes like rogan josh, or methi chicken in order to achieve authentic flavour expression. Onion "freshens" spice. Its inclusion will work against you when cooking to create dense and warm aromas. For instance I would never use onion in paneer. In our tradition this is a dish designed to be soft, and nuanced, and onion disturbs that aromatic outcome. Try using leek instead of onion in a homemade roasted tomato soup for a richer, warmer and sweeter result. Similarly stick to just garlic in a ragu and see the difference the absence of onion makes: it will feel like "cuddlier" flavour. On the flip side, using bucketloads of onion can create very intense sweet flavour. A classic Afghani dish uses two kilos of mince with one kilo of chopped onion that's pressure cooked with paprika, black pepper, tomato, salt, and turmeric for forty-five minutes. It yields an incredibly aromatic kebab dish with echoing sweet and astringent flavour that you'll still be tasting the next day—in a good way! Pair these kebabs with flat breads and a pickled vegetable salad for a complete experience.

Quantity:
One-half to two onions in dishes feeding four to six people.

Use with:
Tomato. Cumin seed. Mustard oil. Turmeric powder. Kashmiri chilli powder. Ginger powder. Green cardamom pods. Cinnamon quills. Tamarind.

Replace with:
Asafoetida OR a combination of nigella seed and garlic.

Pepper Black

Category:
Hot spice.

Profile:
Black pepper is harvested as a fruit from the peppercorn vine. When it's dried, black pepper loses its obvious fruity aroma and shows all of its dark side. Its specific profile shifts depending on the nature of the grind. This is because spice form has an enormous impact on its aromatic expression. Fine black pepper is **gritty** and has a **dark soil** heat: imagine fine dirt still warm from beneath an old campfire. Cracked black pepper presents texturally as a **round boulder** with a **pebbled heat**: this form is more akin to stones surrounding the camp fire deeply warmed by flame that hold heat for a longer time.

Form:
Rough circular peppercorns can range in colour from black to silver to brick or maroon.

IN COOKING:
I love profiling "common" aromatics: even the mundane is sacred when it comes to spice. In Western culinary cultures black pepper is ubiquitous alongside salt. But travel to the East and black pepper takes on a far more exotic role. In a masala, the gritty texture of black pepper is an important contrast to sweeter and prettier aromatic spices. For example, black pepper makes cinnamon powder spicier and sweeter, clove bud warmer and less medicinal, and ginger powder rounder. Versions of back pepper chicken exist across the regions of Southern India where black pepper is grown, commonly pairing black pepper with fresh garlic, fresh ginger, and whole green chillies to produce a dry and resonant "hot-rock" heat. Use black pepper in regional Southern Indian or Sri Lankan dishes to inflame the humid quality of fresh chilli, or in Central Indian dishes to emphasise the drier aromatic heat. You can even take black pepper out of its table shaker and use the fine ground form in desserts: fine ground black pepper matches well with strawberries, or with milk chocolate.

QUANTITY:
One-quarter to one-half teaspoon in dishes feeding four to six people.

Use with:
Red chilli powder. Fresh turmeric. Cinnamon quill. Cassia powder. Fresh ginger. Curry leaf. Lemongrass. Cumin powder.

Replace with:
Course ground white pepper.

Also called:
Kali mirch.

Pepper White

Category:
Hot spice.

Profile:
White peppercorns are a very different spice to black in terms of aromatic presentation. This is the softer, less angular expression of dried peppercorn heat. White peppercorn as a finely ground aromatic has notes of **warmed earth** and **dried hay**. Secondary aromas reach into **flint**—the end taste leaves a very faint and fine **metallic residue**.

Form:
Textured circular peppercorns ranging in colour from pale cream to silver to pale yellow/tan.

In cooking:
I don't come across many who have white pepper in their regular spice roster. It took me a while to work with it regularly, too. But now I reach for it whenever I want

to add a note of refined elegance. My favourite use of fine white pepper is alongside dried chilli in traditional Kashmiri Pandit dishes: white pepper draws forward the floral quality in *hot* category spices, softening the bite of dried chilli into something prettier. Likewise combining fine white pepper with cracked black pepper fills in and smooths out the hot "boulder" heat of black pepper when "gritty" is not the desired outcome. Try using black and white peppers together when seasoning any savoury dish to contribute interest and texture. Chefs often use white pepper in cream-based sauces so as not to disturb the soft colour and flavour. I love to use a little fine white pepper in my pavlova to draw out a savoury sweetness from the rich meringue.

Quantity:
One-quarter to one-half teaspoon in dishes feeding four to six people.

Use with:
Kashmiri chilli powder. Coriander leaf. Clove buds. Cinnamon quill. Fresh turmeric. Fresh ginger. Coconut oil. Fennel seed. Fennel powder.

Replace with:
Szechuan pepper.

Also called:
Safed mirch.

Pepper Szechuan

Category:
Hot spice.

Profile:
Perhaps one of the more interesting varieties of peppercorn, Szechuan pepper is a complex profile that's really very pretty. Initial primary characters of **spicy pot pourri** give way to **sugared mint**. The heat in Szechuan pepper is a secondary character and comes through as a **mild peppermint heat.**

Form:
A round and pale pinkish-green peppercorn with the appearance of a budding rose.

In cooking:
There are all sorts of ways to get the best out of Szechuan pepper. Use it in a classic bouillabaisse to add a floral

heat that complements the seafood stew's rustic aroma. My dad loved pairing Eastern spice with classic French dishes and this is one of those possibilities. In Kashmiri dishes using a non-traditional spice like Szechuan pepper adds a cache of interest that plays into the known aroma of Kashmiri chilli. Grind Szechuan pepper and use it in a leek tart alongside sour cream, salt, tarragon, onion, and a little fine white pepper. Grind the peppercorns and blend with amchur, a little fresh green chilli, salt, and lime for a super tangy dish of fried Szechuan peppercorn shrimp. Use Szechuan pepper in winter soups for a mild pepper kick.

Quantity:
A quarter to a half teaspoon in dishes feeding four to six people.

Use with:
Indian bay leaf. Jaggery. Fresh ginger. Coconut milk. Garlic. Fresh red chilli. Fresh galangal. Fresh turmeric.

Replace with:
Equal parts course ground white pepper and Kashmiri chilli powder.

Pomegranate Molasses

CATEGORY:
Acidic spice.

PROFILE:
Pomegranate molasses is a syrup made from the seeds of the pomegranate fruit. It's not a pure spice in that sugar is added to the process, but to be honest that sweetness is part of the charm. Pomegranate molasses has upfront primary characters: the syrup is **acrid**, **bitter**, and **sweet,** with a **tart cranberry** taste and a tail of **sweet syrup**. It passes straight from primary to tertiary character, the later relating to the syrup's **viscosity**—the texture of pomegranate molasses thickens the spice bed, which translates to an overall richer mouthfeel.

FORM:
A dark, viscous syrup.

IN COOKING:
Pomegranate molasses is one of those "all dishes, all the time" kind of additions for me. It is *so* delicious. It's a key taste in Middle Eastern dishes, prized for its tart, sweet, and slightly bitter profile. Part of its beauty is its versatility. I use pomegranate molasses in salad dressings alongside olive oil, garlic, and salt and pepper in place of vinegar or lemon juice for a strong and rich dressing on a mesclun leaf salad of sliced red onion, toasted walnuts, and crumbled fresh feta or ricotta. Try it in marinades with fresh ginger, sesame oil, sesame seeds, and a little fresh red chilli. Drizzle pomegranate molasses on meats and vegetables before roasting to aid caramelisation. In a classic masala bed, pomegranate molasses can stand in for tamarind for a slightly "higher tone" aromatic result.

QUANTITY:
One to two teaspoons in dishes feeding four to six people.

USE WITH:
Yellow mustard seed. Mustard oil. Fenugreek leaf. Red chilli powder. Fresh ginger. Ginger powder. Turmeric powder. Cumin seed. Cumin powder. Garam masala.

REPLACE WITH:
Tamarind concentrate OR equal parts tamarind and fresh lime.

Saffron

CATEGORY:
Structural spice.

PROFILE:
Saffron is a spice derived from the flower of the Saffron Crocus Sativa. The filament used in cooking is the dried stigma: hand harvested, this is a delicate spice with a high price tag. Saffron has a complex profile. Primary characters run from a **dry floral heat**, through to **sandalwood** and an aroma of **fresh pressed cotton**. Like pomegranate molasses, saffron skips secondary aromatic expression in favour of a strong tertiary character: it has a **strong**, **upright** and **wooded** structure.

FORM:
Very fine threads that are saffron orange in colour.

IN COOKING:
Saffron threads are magical, but I was a little scared to use them for a long time. Something about the process of soaking the threads before cooking them made its use and application feel complicated. It's really not. A pinch of saffron threads dissolved in a few tablespoons of warm water can be added as a finishing touch to clear stock-based soups: for such a seemingly delicate spice, saffron has a solid structural quality and will provide your soup with a beautiful aromatic frame. A pinch of saffron in a few tablespoons of warm milk can be added back to custards, panna cotta, rice puddings like the traditional Kashmiri-style kheer, and ice-creams to contribute a gentle dry floral-sandalwood aroma and—again—a subtle structure.

QUANTITY:
A pinch of saffron threads in a dish feeding four to six people.

USE WITH:
Rose water. Green cardamom pods. Cream. Vegetable stocks. Leeks.

REPLACE WITH:
Saffron is one of two spices in this Companion that has no equitable replacement, along with Indian black salt.

Salt Indian Black

CATEGORY:
Salt.

PROFILE:
Indian black salt is complex, distinctive and divisive courtesy of its unique primary aromatic character that displays strong tastes of **sulphur**, and **boiled egg**, and segues into the secondary appearance of **seaweed**. Its tertiary character shows in **savoury texture** that is chased by tastes of **chemical butter popcorn** and **shellfish**.

FORM:
A very fine powder that is pale pink or lavender in colour. The "black" in the name refers more to the unrefined salt crystal, which is deep purple, almost black in colour. It is a volcanic salt harvested in the Himalayas then kiln-fired to increase its sulphuric quality.

IN COOKING:
Thinking about Indian black salt as a kind of chicken salt will give you an idea of how to place it in recipes. Its very strong savoury character and lower sodium drive makes this a salt to use to enhance umami and contribute savoury interest to a dish: it works beautifully with a tray of baked chicken, in any dish pairing eggplant and tomato, and its inclusion will reduce the game quality of pork and enhance its meaty sweetness. Indian black salt is a beautiful match with shellfish. Indian black salt should be paired with a primary salt—as I mentioned earlier, this black salt has a low sodium drive therefore is not powerful enough to establish clarified spice tone on its own. If normally using one teaspoon of a sea salt, for example, slightly reduce that quantity to a three-quarter teaspoon, and add a third of a teaspoon of Indian black salt. It is best added during the cooking process of the dish, in order to reduce its sulphuric aroma and enhance its savoury texture.

QUANTITY:
One-third to a three-quarter teaspoon in dishes feeding four to six people.

USE WITH:
Pink salt. Nigella seed. Curry leaf. Fresh green chilli. Turmeric powder. Fenugreek powder. Fennel seed. Amchur. Cassia powder. Clove buds.

Replace with:
Indian black salt is one of two spices in this Companion that has no equitable replacement, along with saffron.

Also called:
Kala namak. Himalayan black salt. Kala loon.

Salt Fine Pink

Category:
Salt.

Profile:
Fine pink salt is such an effervescent experience. It hits the palate with a direct intensity. First up primary taste is intense **sodium** that segues to secondary **mineral** characters and a lively **popping fizz** texture. It has a **round** and **slightly sweet** finish.

Form:
A textural and fine salt grain ranging from palest candy pink to pinkish white in colour.

In cooking:
Fine pink salt is my common go-to in the kitchen. Its fine texture allows the salt to dissolve and disperse across the palate with an "even" quality, meaning it drives companion

aromatics symmetrically, resulting in a classically beautiful flavour expression. The nature of pink salt's aromatic structure gives it a "round" nuance that softens sodium while retaining its drive. Use it when seeking complexity, sweetness, and softness—a favourite kind of aromatic bed. Pink salt is a natural partner to lamb and mutton; it works beautifully with crustaceans and sweet, thick-fleshed white fish; and it is a prettier alternative to fine white salt when used as a table salt.

QUANTITY:
One teaspoon to one-and-a-third teaspoons in dishes feeding four to six people.

USE WITH:
Tomatoes. Onion. Garlic. Ajwain. Turmeric powder. Black cardamom pods. Fresh fenugreek leaf.

REPLACE WITH:
Equal parts fine white sea salt and fleur de sel (white flake salt).

ALSO CALLED:
Namak.

Salt Fine White Sea

CATEGORY:
Salt.

PROFILE:
Fine white sea salt is the classic "salty" salt. If someone were to ask you what salt tastes like, this is the experience you would imagine. A fine white sea salt runs a straight line down the centre of the tongue. It has an **oceanic** primary character that segues to a secondary taste of **soft seaweed**.

FORM:
A textural, fine salt grain generally appearing as clean white in colour.

IN COOKING:
A fine white sea salt offers the most classical interpretation of salt usage. It has a heavy sodium drive and a

"linear" appearance in the mouth. It is very direct, and strong. I use fine white salt when working with produce that tends to flatten spice like beef or skinless, boneless chicken. When used with these proteins, white sea salt makes sure that aromatics are "heard." When it comes to seafood a small quantity of sea salt echoes a quality of ocean fish, but too much will result in sodium dominance. One of my favourite uses of white salt is combining it with a fine pink salt: the white salt is the fabric / skirt and the pink salt is the flounce resulting in an aromatic bed with a clear structure but a little more detail and nuance.

Quantity:
One teaspoon in dishes feeding four to six people.

Use with:
Pomegranate molasses. Fenugreek powder. Fenugreek leaf. Fresh red chilli. Cumin powder. Fennel seed. Fresh ginger. Ginger powder. Jaggery.

Replace with:
Fine white lake salt.

Also called:
Namak.

Sumac

CATEGORY:
Acidic spice.

PROFILE:
Sumac is a dried and ground berry commonly used in Middle Eastern cuisine. It has a slightly coarse texture and a primary character of **coriander powder**, **cardamom**, and **sweet lime**. It has a **subtle salt** secondary character.

FORM:
A granular dried spice with the appearance of rough sand and a striking, distinct dark grape colour.

IN COOKING:
Sumac doesn't have a presence in traditional Indian regional cooking, but that doesn't mean I haven't fallen in love with its lime-y, salty character. Unlike amchur,

sumac has a darker, shadowed aromatic aspect: sumac insists where amchur suggests. But like amchur it is quite delicious when used untempered. Quick and easy uses include sprinkling sumac over salads, fruit salads, flat breads or leavened breads before baking, or as a finishing touch to hummus. Sumac with salt, pepper, fennel seed, and chilli powder is an addictive seasoning for honey roasted nuts. Make the most of its textured and lower tone acidity with delicate grilled or baked fish that are easily overwhelmed by use of fresh lemon and lime. Sumac makes lentils yummier: it can brighten a cassoulet, enhance spice in a channa sabzi, or add interest to breakfast baked beans with some fine black pepper and a little Tabasco.

Quantity:
One-half to one teaspoon in dishes feeding four to six people.

Use with:
Fennel powder. Cumin seed. Turmeric powder. Black pepper. White pepper. White salt. Preserved lemon. Curry leaf.

Replace with:
Amchur is a soft replacement. Tamarind is a strong replacement.

Tamarind

Category:
Acidic spice.

Profile:
Tamarind is a fruit from the tamarind tree: it grows in a brown pod the shape of a pea pod. It's generally pulped and sold in block form. Tamarind has a strong primary character of **sour grass** (oxalis). The pulp has tertiary characters of **wood** and **husk**.

Form:
As a concentrate, tamarind is a dark and rich syrup. In its block form, tamarind appears glossy brown-black with a smooth putty texture.

In cooking:
Tamarind is such a staple of broader Indian and South East Asian cooking. In traditional Kashmiri Pandit cuisine

it features alongside eggplant in a sabzi of tangy brinjal, and also forms one of the core ingredients in kashur gaad; a classic tamarind fish curry. Tamarind adds a striking element to Southeast Asian noodle dishes; it works as a meat tenderiser in marinades; and it gives an extra tart quality when added to chutneys. In traditional regional Indian cooking, tamarind adds beauty and texture to sabzis requiring a tart bite to contrast *hot* and *earthy* aromatic profiles.

QUANTITY:
One teaspoon to one tablespoon in dishes feeding four to six people.

USE WITH:
Fish sauce. Hot red chilli powder. White salt. Fresh coriander. Garam masala. Yellow mustard seed. Black mustard seed. Garlic. Onion. Sesame oil.

REPLACE WITH:
Pomegranate molasses OR equal parts brown vinegar and brown sugar.

Turmeric Fresh

Category:
Bitter spice.

Profile:
Fresh turmeric is a wetter, cooler aromatic experience than turmeric powder. Primary characters are **water chestnut** tailed by a mild bite of **floral pepper heat**. It has a secondary character of **fresh water**, and **soft orange citrus**. Its tertiary shape is **broad** and **wet** like a river delta.

Form:
A tubular rhizome with a dirty beige skin, revealing a vibrant orange interior when cut.

In cooking:
Fresh turmeric has a different contribution than turmeric powder. It is a gentle spice which shows its best face when not in direct contact with heat. The "wet" quality

of fresh turmeric lightens the density of darker or more dense aromatics: consider using it in a beef rendang to freshen the heat of chilli. Add fresh turmeric at the end of winter soups and slow cooks to brighten the dried spice bed. It marries beautifully with clear broths and is a lighter *bitter* addition to scrambled eggs or morning omelettes. Consider grating fresh turmeric into falafel, meatballs, or vegetable patties.

QUANTITY:
One to two teaspoons in dishes feeding four to six people.

USE WITH:
Turmeric powder. Fresh ginger. Pink salt. Fresh green chilli. Yoghurt. Asafoetida. Aniseed.

REPLACE WITH:
Turmeric powder.

ALSO CALLED:
Haldi.

Turmeric Powder

Category:
Bitter spice.

Profile:
Turmeric powder is the ground form of the dried turmeric rhizome. It's very heavy on the tongue, yet equally turmeric powder has a complex and beautiful aromatic profile. Primary characters move through **warm ginger**, **clay**, and **bitter orange rind**. There are secondary **floral** qualities and a faint tail of **fine white pepper**. Tertiary characters relate to its dual textural appearance: both as **heavy clay** on the tongue and a **round powdered** quality through the central mouth space.

Form:
A vivid and distinct "turmeric" yellow powder that is silken and heavy.

IN COOKING:
Turmeric powder is a staple spice in the Indian pantry. Traditionally, turmeric is used to provide an aromatic backbone within a masala rather than as a "forward" taste. My Kashmiri grandmother told me to always add a little sugar to offset the bitterness and my Dad advised a shy hand so the turmeric flavour didn't push through. Like a photo frame draws your eye to certain shapes or colours in the photo, turmeric frames a dish and makes tomatoes taste sweeter, garlic taste brighter, or black pepper taste grittier. Basically use about a third of a teaspoon and your dish is more delicious. Turmeric powder is lovely in a summer passata, zucchini fritters, or a broth-based soup or dumpling bowl. It makes an omelette richer. In very small amounts turmeric powder also intensifies or adds colour. I use it for this reason in coconut milk-based seafood dishes.

QUANTITY:
One-quarter to one-half teaspoon in dishes feeding four to six people.

USE WITH:
Kashmiri chilli powder. Coriander powder. Coriander leaf. Amchur. Nigella seed. Fennel seed. Cumin seed. Fresh ginger. Ghee. Green cardamom pods.

REPLACE WITH:
Equal parts ginger powder and fresh turmeric.

ALSO CALLED:
Haldi.

Acknowledgements

My husband Scott was the one who said to me: you don't have to *write* your spice book, you just have to *write it down*. That changed everything. As anyone who's ever written a book knows, the experience can be grinding. My first book—Spirits In A Spice Jar—was published in 2018. The experience of writing it was fraught. I wasn't sure that I wanted to take another turn. But after five years of teaching spice classes I'd had enough people ask me for this book that ignoring the obvious began to seem pretty silly. Scott's words were more than semantics. They freed me to see that agony isn't the mirror experience of creativity. That I already had the information living inside me. Darling, you're my best friend. I love you to the moon and back. I love how you can be so *right* about things, in such an easy manner. So I took your advice. I just wrote it all down.

Thank you to my boys, Cailean and Ash. You guys love books, and words, and puzzles as much as I do. You—

mostly—listen to my endless YouTube spice and recipe videos. But mainly you just love me for me. For being your rainbow-chasing, cheesy-music-loving, kitchen-dancing mum. And that supercharges all of my efforts.

Sarah Date. Jennifer Crescenzo. Lauren Trickett. The three of you have had your hands all over this manuscript and I couldn't be more thankful. Sarah, for your incisive edits for clarity, cohesion, and style. Jen, for knowing me so well you could ask me the questions I hadn't answered and rewrite me when I needed it. Trickers, your proofing ability is unmatched. As is your generosity.

A book cover is one of the toughest asks, and Melinda Orchard you were my total superstar. The best bit about working with forever-friends is that they know exactly who you are, even when you aren't sure yourself. You nailed this cover Nindy. Thank you so much.

Toshi Singh I knew the first time I saw your illustrations that I wanted you in my corner, and your work with me on this book has been so incredible. I love that you took what I gave you and created something truly unique, true to my vision, and just so beautiful.

Chippy Dog. For all my night-time couch cuddles.

Lastly thank you to Julie-Ann and her team at Pickawoowoo Publishing. Your guidance on this project has been pinpoint specific. It made the journey easier. Thank you.

Author

Sarina Kamini is a Kashmiri-Australian writer and spice mistress based in Margaret River, Western Australia. She has worked as a food critic, journalist, and editor in Melbourne, Paris, Edinburgh, Barcelona, Southern California, and Margaret River. She now teaches spice classes, runs spice events, and produces video content covering traditional recipes and detailed spice education for her YouTube channel. Sarina lives and cooks with her husband, her two sons, and her dog, DJ Chips. Visit her at sarinakamini.com

www.ingramcontent.com/pod-product-compliance
Lightning Source LLC
Chambersburg PA
CBHW040240010526
44107CB00065B/2820